THE *lifestyle* KITCHEN

THE
lifestyle
KITCHEN

THE SECRET INGREDIENT TO CREATING A HAPPY, HARMONIOUS HOME

ROBERT J GUINAN

RƎTHINK PRESS

First published in Great Britain 2017
by Rethink Press (www.rethinkpress.com)

Cover image © Shutterstock / Anna Efetova

Dedicated to my son Jacob

Contents

Preface

Your kitchen needs to be a smart extension of your home. An intelligently designed lifestyle kitchen is the secret ingredient to creating a harmonious, happy home.

We all have a different vision of our dream kitchen. Your dream kitchen may be set in a penthouse apartment with panoramic views of the city skyline, even though you live in a terraced house in a leafy rural village. You might be hankering after a farmhouse kitchen, or maybe you'd prefer a futuristic, streamlined kitchen. Whatever your dream, I promise you that you have my unconditional support. I wish you every success in owning your dream kitchen in your dream location. Please don't be disheartened if you don't have your dream kitchen yet. You're much closer than you think.

The Lifestyle Kitchen

As a child I used to sit under my mum's feet while she mixed the batter for the cake, waiting for the exclusive privilege of the seasoned cake taster – licking the bowl. My brother and I would get an electric beater each and hold them like lollipops, scouring every last millimetre with our tongues, hunting out the delicious batter. As a professional, I have been in and around kitchens for the best part of fourteen years. I left school at 16 years' old and I learned to be a chef. I started as a commis chef in a beautiful country club that had three different restaurants. I had many opportunities to learn from some wonderfully talented head chefs. The French head chef, Eric, was an inspiration. In the kitchen he moved with such grace and artisan flair, but he ran a tight ship and second rate was never tolerated. He would say to me, 'Robeeaar, you are only as good as your last dish. You must learn from your mistakes and improve on your weaknesses.' These words have carried me through to this day.

I'm sure you have many memories set in a kitchen. Perhaps when you first cooked for your partner, or when you opened a letter to find out you had been accepted to your chosen college or university. Maybe a moment with your son or daughter when you realised they're not your little girl or boy any more. Whatever those memories are, it's no coincidence that the kitchen is the setting for them.

In this book I hope to enlighten, provoke and challenge your thoughts around the kitchen so you can set up a room in which you can create many more wonderful memories with the people you love the most.

If you have picked up this book it tells me one thing about you – you've had enough of your under-performing kitchen and you want a change. Thank you for trusting me to help you; I want to repay that trust by serving you. I love the kitchen and what it stands for. For me, it's a symbol of community and the foundation of a happy, healthy home. A kitchen creates a sense of belonging, security and peace of mind. It's what makes a house feel like a home.

In the last ten years I've seen one problem plenty of times – you want to turn the kitchen into the heart of your home, but somehow it still lacks a beat. Your kitchen doesn't have rhythm or soul. Read this book so you can take your kitchen from where it is now and to where you want it to be. You can reach that ideal you have in your mind's eye of how it will look and, more importantly, how it will feel.

Introduction

I believe that when you change your kitchen you're looking for more than just cosmetic change – you're looking to change the dynamics of your home. I dive deep with my clients, pushing past the visible, obvious needs to find out what the true driving force is for the change. This is our 'why', which gives us focus and clarity. The 'why' gives us a reason to do what we do and achieve the outcomes we want.

When I was 'cheffing' my hobby was racing road bikes on short circuits, such as the iconic Brands Hatch, Silverstone and Donnington racecourses. But motor sport is an expensive hobby. I needed to bridge the gap between my wages and my tyre bill, so I got a second job sweeping the floor in a local kitchen and joinery workshop. When I was racing bikes, someone told me that you go where you focus. It's painfully obvious. You need to find that special 'why' to give you the focus that will help you change your kitchen to achieve the feeling you want. If you follow the process set out in this book, it will help you find your 'why'. Jump through to the sections that are most critical to you, but some of the ideas follow on from a previous section, so it's worth going back through the book chapter by chapter.

Three common problems

First, we need to identify the problems with your kitchen. The problems I share here are the three most common ones, and you need to consider them as part of the process.

1. LACK OF FUNCTIONALITY. Having things in the wrong place at the wrong time can be a problem. Most kitchens fitted in the last twenty years probably follow the 'working triangle' layout, so when I say 'in the wrong place' I mean 'in the wrong place for you'.

- Maybe the oven is at the wrong height for you to comfortably use, or you don't have enough storage solutions.

- You might have too many deep cupboards, so food gets

stacked up and you have to move everything in the cupboard to get to the items at the back.

- Have you ever been out shopping and bought something that you thought you needed, like a tin of tomatoes, only to find when you were storing them that you already had six tins, in three different varieties – chopped, plum and passata – hidden at the back of the cupboard?

- Maybe you don't have enough worktop space. Prepping for a meal is half the battle of cooking. Do you have enough room to slice, dice and julienne your vegetables? Do you have space to roll out pastry for a pie?

- You might not even have enough space to be able to plate up the dinner. Plates get stacked on top of each other or are left teetering on the edge. They could be knocked off at any moment, leaving your efforts splashed across the floor and the dog lapping up the remnants of your masterpiece of a roast.

2. BAD DESIGN. The design of the kitchen can be a problem. This is a huge area, and it means different things to different people, at different stages of their lives.

- That maple kitchen that you inherited when you bought your new home is way past its prime now.

- High gloss is fine, but maybe it's not quite 'you' or it's not modern enough now.

- Perhaps you'd love a bit more colour and expression of your character and personality throughout the home.

- Is a good design for you a slab door without handles? Or do you prefer the shaker style?

- You might have one of these styles already and be desperate to swap it for an alternative.

- Maybe your pockets or chunky knitwear get caught on the handles and all you seem to do is accidentally open drawers and doors.

- Perhaps your kitchen doesn't let you entertain in the way you wish it would. Are you fed up of your guests being schmoozed with nibbles and drink by your partner while you slave in the kitchen?

3. GETTING IT DONE. The execution of your grand design

can be a problem. Choosing the right people and companies can be a minefield.

- How do you know you're not going to get ripped off? You see all these programmes on television about shady, underhand cowboys taking advantage, promising the earth but then riding off into the sunset leaving the job unfinished. Your hard-earned money has been frittered away on poor workmanship and cheap products.

- Even more off-putting is when you order your kitchen only to find that things are missing or out of stock, leaving you to phone up to find out when a replacement item will be delivered.

If any of these are your fears, this book will help you identify the rogues from the professionals. It's the few who ruin it for the many. Read on and you'll have the confidence that you have made an informed, well-judged decision.

I don't want to be negative. I want you to know I understand your concerns and we will work together so that you get that perfect lifestyle kitchen. I understand that you've waited and saved your money so that you can get it right. I want you to get your dream kitchen.

All shapes and sizes

I love working with every type of client, because I love problem-solving. Every potential customer has a different objective. When I went to see Mary and her partner Charlie, her specific concern was her glasses. Mary has an extraordinary depth of knowledge about wine and has a beautiful collection of glassware. As this was a massive part of her world, she wanted her glasses on show. They were a reminder of wonderful afternoons and evenings spent with friends and family. These glasses held her memories.

Another client, George, was fanatical about art. He wanted to dedicate wall space to a piece that he was going to get commissioned after his new kitchen was fitted. We came up with a solution that George was inspired by. We used some floating feature shelving with recessed LED lighting. This lighting would shine down on the newly created art work.

The main chef or cook of the home is mentioned often in this book. We live in a modern world, and men and women both cook in the home. I'm a man and I love to cook, and I love to cook with my wife and my daughter. I talk about partners in the book – girlfriends, boyfriends, husbands and wives. If you're in a great place in your head and your heart and you don't have a partner, please don't be offended by my references to partners. Maybe you've just moved into your first home. You might be enjoying your freedom and independence, hosting parties and gatherings for friends and family. This book will help you to create an open-plan kitchen and living space for those occasions.

Grandparents, I hear your voices too. While your children may have flown the nest years ago and may even have started their own families, with young or even teenage children, this book is still for you. I'll help you create a space that fits your lifestyle – somewhere that stays true to your personality but caters for your children and grandchildren. Let's create a multi-purpose room.

For couples, partners and singles who don't have children, there is content in this book that is relevant to you. I have written this book for people who want to make more memories with the people they most care about, whatever their stage in life.

Developers, I include you in the fold with a heartfelt welcome. I completely understand that it's a numbers game and you want to get the most from your investment. You want your properties to appeal to as many people as possible to increase sales of your houses. I hope you find value in this book and that you can apply the principles to new projects.

Chapter 1

THE SEVEN MISTAKES

1. Making do

My friend Stephen's mother-in-law, Mercia, has been talking about getting a new kitchen for the best part of six years. The doors are discoloured and the vinyl is starting to peel off. A couple of the hinges have come loose and the doors barely hang on to the cabinets any more. She's been in the market for a new kitchen for a good while. Stephen's wife, Beth, is one of four siblings, and the whole family always goes round to Mercia's house for Sunday lunch. Every week, there could be up to twelve hungry adults and children round for dinner.

The sisters tend to pile into the kitchen to help with preparing the food and take it in turns to stir the gravy, but there is barely enough space to swing a yo-yo, let alone fit in five adults.

Stephen said to Mercia, 'Why don't you open up the space and create a bigger kitchen?' Mercia was worried and thought it would be far too expensive to do that. And so the cycle continues, and Mercia continues to make do.

You don't know what you don't know, so what's the harm in finding out? Most building companies offer a no-obligation quote, and at least by getting some quotes you know the facts. Of course, get three quotes so you can compare. It may cost more than you think or it may be less, but without progressing you will never know.

2. Kitchen planners

Having made the decision to change your kitchen, what's the first thing you do? Maybe you do a Google search and find your nearest kitchen retailer. You jump in the car and head out for an information-gathering trip. Before the hot air blows into your face as you enter the sliding doors, you have been coerced into sitting down with a planner and designing your kitchen.

I don't encourage this. The planners have efficient software for creating kitchen layouts, but problems arise when it starts becoming a game of Tetris. Remember Tetris? You had to put set shapes in a logical order so they would all fit nice and neatly. Of course, you want things in your kitchen to fit nice and neatly, but what about those set shapes? Kitchen units come in groups of hundreds of millimetres – for example 300mm, 500mm or 600mm. There are some half-sizes, like 350mm and 450mm. Planners like simplicity, but in the ten years I've been in this profession I've never come across a 'simple' room size. On-site measurements are never square and true. Creating a layout to the nearest millimetre looks great on a computer screen, but it doesn't translate well when it comes to installation.

3. Generic lighting

When extending a kitchen, people often employ the services of a builder. Typically, you bring in a builder to create the room and space you desire. Usually, when the space is about two-thirds completed you start to think about the kitchen. Most builders will advise you on the costs of the build before they start, and give you a quote. The builder will bring in a team of contractors to carry out the work. By the time you get two-thirds of the way into the build, the electricians have run the first phase of all the electrical cabling to where it is needed. Once the extension has been wired, the contractors do the dry lining and board the walls, followed by the plastering.

If you bring in a kitchen designer at this late stage, the builders will already have put a generic lighting plan in place. The designer's ideas for ambient lighting would have to be retrofitted – to make changes at this stage will involve more cost, disruption and 'making good' (re-plastering and decorating). Most people pass up the opportunity to add a better lighting system to avoid the hassle.

4. You, but not you

I enjoy reading magazines – it's a massive part of understanding and evaluating ideas to add to my toolbox. Pinterest is a global phenomenon because it allows users to share ideas they have 'pinned'. The images we consume in the media have been carefully crafted to leave a lasting impression.

When you go clothes shopping and walk into a department store, you might see an outfit you like on a mannequin. I frequently do too. But sometimes it turns out that I don't have the right body type to pull off that look or I don't feel confident in it. Instead, I buy what fits with my character type.

Your kitchen is no different. If a kitchen looks amazing in a picture (which it will) that's great, but make sure it's true to you, your style and your home.

5. Paint by numbers

Do you remember paint by numbers when you were younger? All the sections labelled number 3 had to be painted blue, number 7 painted red and so on. It gave us comfort and pleasure, it was easy to understand and if we followed the key, our picture was going to look as it should.

We might have a favourite colour and want to use that in our kitchen design. Believe me, colour is not the issue – tones and textures are. I have seen some stunning all-white kitchens. How the textures and tones are used makes all the difference.

If you don't want your kitchen to look outdated in a few years, read on!

6. Apples and pears

Which is heavier – a ton of bricks or a ton of feathers? You know they both weigh the same, but how do you know which is the better kitchen unit, door, handle, drawer or worktop?

You now have the headache of ascertaining what is a good price for the product. White base units are all the same, aren't they? Can you be sure that they are? If you have two units that look the same but are wildly different in price, how can you possibly know which to go for? Is price an important factor for you? Does it even matter about the differences? Some companies spend millions to tell you it doesn't, and others stake their reputation on telling you that it does.

7. How hard can it be?

I like golf, and I like to watch major golf tournaments like the Ryder Cup on television. It's easy, right? You have a tiny white ball that you knock about with a little stick – how hard can it be? I openly admit I'm a novice at golf and playing it is a hundred times harder than the pros make it look. Why? Well, I didn't dedicate my life to practising every day, perfecting the techniques and using the latest tools to make me a pro. We admire people like sports stars, actors and celebrities because they make something look easy – they are more than just good at it.

If you think fitting a kitchen is just putting boxes against the wall, that's like saying an accountant is just good at counting. If you value your time, get a professional in – they will do it more quickly, tidily and efficiently than you can.

But how can you tell a good fitter from a bad one? If you had three installation quotes and they were all the same cost, how would you pick one? The colour of their work boots? Flip a coin? Read on to find out, and you'll never need your poker face again when it comes to choosing a contractor.

Chapter 2

THE SEVEN SOLUTIONS

1. Evaluate the space

Evaluating the space you have to work with is crucial. Know your options and the restrictions around planning permission that might apply.

There are three main options:

1. Use the existing area and re-configure it to suit your needs.

2. Knock a wall through, combining two rooms to make a larger room.

3. Add an extension to the back or side of the house to give you the space you want.

People lean towards option one if they don't want to add to the disruption and building costs. The ultimate easy win is to knock a non-supporting wall down, combining two rooms to give you that open-plan space. You then have a blank canvas for planning how you use this area.

2. Get a kitchen designer

Bring in a kitchen designer at the earliest possible stage. Working with you and an architect, they will help you to stay on top of your budgeting. They'll work through ideas to come up with a layout that your chosen contractors can use to quote accurately, rather than submitting a provisional sum. This prevents the dreaded paralysis caused by running out of budget, which is more common than you might think. It is easy to get lured in with a low provisional sum which may cover the very basics. Once work has started and you finally pick the eventual fixtures and fitting, you can receive a much larger bill than you had allowed for. Working to fixed costs puts you in control of what you're doing and how you go about doing it. The reason we start any project is to achieve the desired outcome.

3. Think lighting

Lighting is often overlooked or considered at the wrong time. Appropriate lighting will change the look and feel of a space, and I'm not just talking about under-cabinet lighting. There are three types of lighting:

1. NATURAL – provided by windows and doors.

2. TASK – the main room lighting; for example, ceiling LED spot lights.

3. AMBIENT – such as under-cabinet lighting or feature lighting on plinths or handle rails.

Lighting can dramatically influence your emotional connection to a room. You don't need to flood a room with light, either. Clever and subtle lighting gives a classy and elegant finish to a room, no matter what style you use.

4. Social interaction

Take time to understand your entertaining style. When you have friends and family over, do you prefer having the dishes in the middle of the table with everyone helping themselves, or would you rather dish up individual plates, more like in a restaurant? The first option may be more suited to a booth-style seating, close and intimate, while the second would need a large dining table.

The dining or lounge area sometimes gets forgotten or considered as an afterthought. Open-plan living is a whole package, and only you know what your intentions are for this space. Consider how you interact with others to make sure you get the most use out of the space you want to create.

5. Be design-led, not product-led

Product-led companies use discounts to entice customers. This will affect your experience, as you may find that the planners have limitations based on that range or style. In contrast, design-led companies use bespoke manufacturers to ensure the space is used as efficiently as possible. A designer can find practical solutions for technically challenging corners, room shapes and ergonomic issues. Product-led companies have a large stock to sell, so they may be more focused on their targets and objectives than on your needs.

6. Colours matter

Taste and style are so personal, but good designers understand how to use trends and colours to give you something unique and personal. A popular styling tip would be to use a neutral colour as the base and include bespoke features and cookware for accents of colour.

For example, you might use a painted glass splashback and match the hue or colour with your kettle, toaster, and coffee, tea and sugar jars. If you're combining your kitchen with a lounge or living area, you could use coloured cushions to tie the two areas together.

7. Execute smarter

A project manager saves you time and money. There's no need to chase contractors or stay in to take deliveries. There's one point of contact, from start to finish, to orchestrate a stress-free renovation project. Bringing in a project manager is the most efficient way to buy your time back.

The human brain can comfortably handle seven tasks at any time. Add running a complex and mentally taxing refurbishment project to the seven tasks you already have on your mind and you're on a fast track to meltdown.

Steve Jobs, ex-Chairman and Founder of Apple, would wear the same clothes day after day so that he didn't have to think about what to put on. This freed up his mental capacity to focus on bringing a technical revolution to the world.

Now you know the seven mistakes and my seven solutions, keep these in mind as I walk you through the HOME system for creating your dream lifestyle kitchen.

Chapter 3

THE HOME SYSTEM

The **HOME** system helps you concentrate on the basics, avoid the seven mistakes and get to the seven solutions faster. Using my **HOME** framework, you will discover the key ingredients to find more Harmony, get more Organised, create the right Mood and choose the best Equipment to enjoy your perfect kitchen with family and friends. In this chapter we'll look at social dynamics, ergonomic layout, cooking patterns, colours, styles and trends, appliances, lighting, budgeting and project completion.

Harmony

Creating an agreeable, orderly arrangement of all the parts of the kitchen will give you structure, open up spaces for the family to come together, improve the social dynamics when entertaining and help you be a better cook.

In music, harmony is the combination of tones and the blending of chords to create something pleasing to the ear. It's the space between the notes that creates the beauty – without the spaces there would be no music. It's the same for our open-plan lifestyle kitchen – the spaces we open up will make the whole room better.

Spatial awareness

How much space do you need to create your dream kitchen? Ask ten people what's the perfect size for a kitchen and you'll get eleven different answers – because you have your own idea of the perfect sized kitchen too. I love and hate this question. It's up there with 'How long is a piece of string?'

My wife and I enjoy watching Netflix, especially the shows set in central New York. My *dream* kitchen would be set on the thirtieth floor, in a four-thousand-square-foot apartment, with panoramic views. By stark contrast, my *perfect* kitchen is in our three-bedroomed, semi-detached house in a small Bedfordshire village. It's perfect because we've squeezed every last ounce out of the space available to us. It's not size that matters, but what you do with it. Think about what you have to use and more importantly, what you want most out of the space.

A client, Margaret and her elderly mother, Tabby, came to see me. They a had a room of 2.4 metres by 2.1 metres. There were no options to extend the kitchen or knock through into another room. The brief from Tabby was to increase the worktop surface area and add appliances to make life more convenient for her. We designed a space that had a fridge/freezer, high-level oven, built-in microwave, dishwasher, washing machine and 5.5 linear metres of worktop.

This was an exceptional case, but it proves that even with the most challenging of sizes you can find a design to suit you.

Remember when I told you that you need to understand your 'why'? When you know the 'why', the 'how' can be figured out. What do you want out of your kitchen and living space? With open plan, the desire for space, light and expanse can look cold and dysfunctional if it isn't focused around the 'why' for your new kitchen.

I want an island in my kitchen

Many people want an island in their kitchen. There's no getting away from the fact that if you want an island in your open-plan kitchen you need a certain amount of space. The most important measurement is the width of the room. If you have a room width of 3000mm (3 metres) an island is possible, but it might not provide the benefits you want. The space for people to move around the island will be holding the island to ransom. I always include a walkway that's at least 900mm wide. That feels most natural. It is a space that doesn't make you feel claustrophobic and it makes the path feel open. Two adults can pass each other side-on.

To put this into context, a standard door opening between two rooms is 686mm–762mm. You wouldn't want to pass another adult through that door side-on. Obviously, you can fit though the door facing forward without any problem, and you could argue that the walkway around the island could be made this same width. My counter to this argument is purely practical. If you had a bag of shopping in one hand, you'd have to turn to the side to walk past the island. Shuffling with heavy bags isn't fun and it's not ideal from a posture point of view. Resentment would slowly build up about the island eating so much into the width of the walkway.

Let's take an example of our room with a width of 3000mm. The width of the walkway would be two times the minimum of 900mm, which is 1800mm. The size of the island is the width of the room minus the walk route, making it 1200mm. That's not a bad width for a non-functional island, but it would have its restrictions if it was a working island. More about this later.

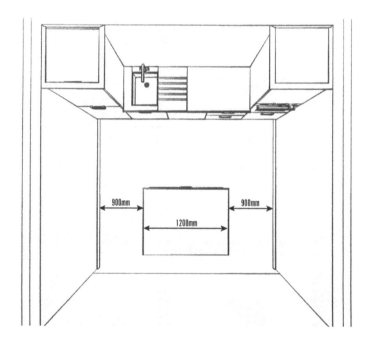

Here's another example. In a kitchen with a horseshoe or C layout, the size of the island is based on the same formula, accounting for the width of the base units down both sides. Standard depths of worktops in the UK are 600mm, except for a few manufacturers who produce their own sizes to match their base units.

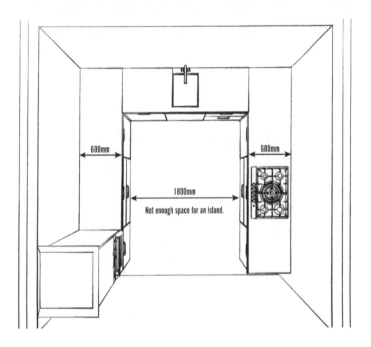

To achieve an island width of 1200mm, which we recognise is a good starting point for an island size, we would need the room to be another 1200mm wider.

Island = room width − base units − walk route

= 4200mm − 1200mm (2 × 600mm) − 1800mm (2 × 900mm)

These are the most basic formulas for working out the size of an island in a new kitchen space. If you don't have the physical space and more worktop surface is one of the most important things for you, a **peninsula** design could work better for you.

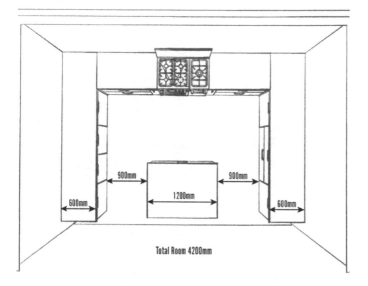

Think about a peninsula

In the kitchen industry we refer to a run of units projecting into the room as a peninsula. Using the first example, we could gain another 900mm of worktop and still have the walk route on the opposite side.

Peninsula = room width – single walk route.

2100mm = 3000mm – 900mm

Even with a horseshoe-shaped room, our second example, using a 3000mm wide room, could have a peninsula of 1500mm. A peninsula can give you a lot more worktop space in the same sized room.

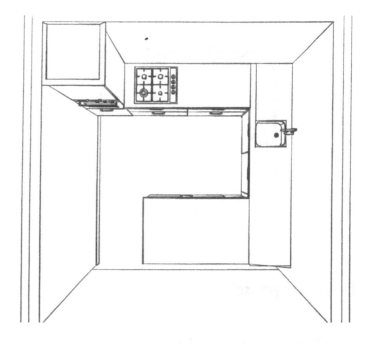

So, when considering the space you have available, don't get caught up with the fashionable island design – consider if a peninsula could work for you. The island might be a nicety rather than a necessity if installing one is at the expense of worktop space!

A modest yet effective island size is about 1500mm wide and 900mm deep. Why these sizes? Symmetry, for one. A 500mm cupboard is a good size – you can fit most large or bulky food processors into it. If you have three cupboards, the doors will all be the same size, making it pleasing to look at. Two people could comfortably work side by side. And the depth allows for bar stools at the back.

Socialising

The kitchen island is more than a fixed piece of furniture. Most people want it to double up on its purpose. Of course, you want worktop and storage space, and nine out of ten islands will have an overhang or a knee well so that you can sit on a bar stool to chat with the chef or cook. This is the image portrayed in articles, social media and magazines, but I don't think it's quite right for most people.

I believe that my industry is misleading you about what the island does for you. We probably agree that the island is important for aesthetic and functional reasons, but I'd like you to consider how an island serves emotional purposes.

About five years ago I read an article about the four human needs, written by Tony Robbins. I then went on to read his book, *Unleash the Power Within*, which I highly recommend. I'll summarise the four human needs, with special attention to how you can achieve them with your kitchen.

1. We have an itch, a need, to have certainty in our lives. The certainty that you'll get paid at the end of the month or get picked up by a friend to go out, and the certainty that when you flick a switch in the home the light comes on. With certainty comes confidence and assurance.

2. Everything has an equal and opposite reaction, so we also have the need for uncertainty – or variety. If we knew what was going to happen all the time, we would get bored. Probably some of your favourite nights out happened on the spur of the moment, with no planning, just making the most of what you have. This variety is a need.

3. The third human need is significance. Significance can be gained in many ways. Do you have a tough boss or manager, someone who is always trying to impose their authority on the situation? They do this because they want to feel important and respected. You may have a friend who's a chronic moaner, who complains the supermarket was so busy, there were no trolleys, they

had to carry all their shopping in their arms and wait three hours at the tills. They need to tell you how bad their experience was to focus the conversation on their problems and give them the significance they are after. Helping out at their local church or charity gives people the significance of doing rewarding work.

4. And finally, we need to connect with other human beings, or more commonly we need love. We need a connection with a parent, sibling, spouse or partner, and friends. The feeling of being wanted and loved is hugely important to our well-being and health.

I believe that when a kitchen island meets your human needs you'll feel more complete as a person and be in harmony with your surroundings. Not convinced? Hear me out…

1. CERTAINTY. You know where the island is, as it's not going to move. If it's a working island with a hob or sink, when you're using the hob you will certainly be at the island, or once everyone has finished cooking or eating you'll clean up at the sink. You can also be certain about where everything is in the drawers, where the pots, pans, knives, flour, pasta and pulses are stored.

2. VARIETY. The adventure of cooking something different, for different people who may have varied dietary require-

ments, hits our need for variety. You might have cooked mushroom risotto a hundred times but it may come out different this time round. You may have an off-day or use a different brand of rice that gives you a different result.

3. SIGNIFICANCE. Like a DJ high up on the stage, you are being looked to for what's coming next, what you have in store, what beat you are about to drop. The chef at the island will get significance no matter what the crowd – children, partners, family or friends. They are looking to you and what you are cooking, wondering how long it'll be until they can eat. What a thrilling way to feel wanted and desired.

4. CONNECTION. Lastly, the bar stools at the island give you a connection to others. You have someone sitting close by and you're able to engage with them.

I think that an island should be designed with these four needs in mind, but it should also be designed to cater for a few extra needs. Those needs are specific to our characteristics. I believe the island should have both bar-stool seating and a small amount of booth-style of seating to give us a connection. You might not have the space for a booth and a dining table, but if you do I urge you to consider my rationale.

Building and improving connections

If you have an island, men are more likely to either stand at the worktop or sit on the stools when in the company of other men. As the saying goes, "brothers in arms standing shoulder to shoulder". Men tend to like to be at the same eye level. So if you're a male chef entertaining male friends, you'll be standing but your friends will want to feel that they're on your level. By sitting shoulder to shoulder, men will relax more as it reduces any sense of competition.

Think about when you're having a beer in a pub. You're more likely to stand at the bar or perch at a tall table than sit down. This is because many men like to be shoulder to shoulder rather than face to face. As a generality, men do not prioritise eye contact in a social environment.

This is somewhat different for woman. In a one-on-one situation bar stools will work well for women also. The user of the kitchen and her female companion will be able to maintain eye contact while chatting and carrying out tasks.

Let's imagine you have an island with a hob and three bar stools that are parallel to the hob. You have three female friends round and they sit on the stools. You as the chef can enjoy seeing all your friends and they can see you. The downside is that your three friends can't easily see each other, so there is a loss of intimacy between them.

Think about this: four women go to dinner and sit at a table, Laura next to Sally and Rachel next to Annie. They have a meal and enjoy a catch up. A few days later, Rachel and Annie both contact Laura and mention that they were a little worried about Sally. Sally didn't seem to be herself the other night. Laura hadn't picked up on that because she hadn't been able to read Sally's facial expressions in such detail.

Seeing into people's eyes helps us read a situation, and that's why I love to design semi-circle booths – everyone can maintain eye contact at the same time. This produces more engagement and connection with friends and family.

Cooking and entertaining styles

Most people, when thinking about an open-plan kitchen, want a big island so they can interact with guests when cooking and feel part of the evening. The media tells you that this is what you should want and need. But is it really what *you* want? Your dream kitchen may be open plan, but what does open plan mean to you? Write it down. Answer these questions:

- I have always dreamt of using the space like...so that I can do...

- I will not put up with...any longer because I do not have...

- It would mean the world to me to be able to...so that I can...

Please take ten minutes to answer these questions for yourself. Once you know the 'why', the 'how' will figure itself out. If you think I'm being obsessive about this, then know that I take what I do seriously and give it the respect it deserves.

For me, open plan is a reconnection to a feeling, a person, a freedom or an expression of character.

If open plan means engagement while entertaining, fantastic. But engagement with whom, exactly? Is it your immediate family, close friends, colleagues from work? Is it your neighbours? Who are these people you want more engagement with?

My dear mum has a heart of gold, and she always wants to be helpful. She goes on two main holidays a year and usually does the driving. She has a large car with a big boot so she can fit in all her luggage. When her car gave up the ghost and went to the great car park in the sky, she was convinced she needed a new large car with a big boot. I asked her why and she said, 'So I have space for all the luggage.'

I asked her, 'Yes, Mum, but are you a professional taxi service?' She responded with a no. 'And remind me, Mum, how many times a year you go away and need all this boot space?'

'Twice.'

'Twice. So what about the other 363 days of the year? Would it not be more suitable to have a nice little run-around?'

My mum's a bit of a sun worshipper – she loves to be in the garden with the warm rays beating down on her face, so a convertible would be perfect. It didn't make sense for her to cater for the couple of days a year when she needs a big boot, when the car's everyday use would be different.

An open-plan kitchen shouldn't be planned around 'what if?' Not in the beginning. It should be planned around what it is, so you can enjoy your home as much as possible and squeeze every last drop out of what the space can be to you.

Dickie bow or jeans and a top?

What is your preferred style of occasion? Do you prefer dinner parties with lots of courses or à la carte cooking? Are you serving up a sorbet palate cleanser and cheese and biscuits, or do you cook it up, serve it in the middle and let everyone take what they like? Fajita wraps and salads, or roast dinners for the five hundred with all the trimmings?

I love both styles. I love the formality of fine dining, with elegance and grace in the cooking and the atmosphere. My childhood hero was Jamie Oliver, and I love his style of cooking too, putting everything in the middle – the camaraderie, the noise, the fuss, the hustle and bustle.

Whichever you prefer will change the dynamic of your open-plan living space. If you prefer a more refined catering style then your space is more likely to have a traditional dining table, with one seat per setting and the option to extend the table for the more salubrious events when you have twelve, sixteen or twenty people to cater for. For the more relaxed style of cooking with the pots in the middle, I think a booth works well, either built into the island or built as its own entity in the room. A booth can make use of a tight or awkward space. It can be built to specific dimensions to take up every last inch of the available space. It can also double up as storage. I love the fun and closeness of a booth, which complements an informal cooking style. Elbows together, it has a playful innocence. I understand a booth isn't as practical when the person in the middle needs to get up to go to the loo, but I think that's part of its charm.

Dining tables can be fun and playful too, and more bench-style seating is appearing in the market. Maybe a chunky oak or upcycled pine table, with a bench seat one side and chairs the other. It's a respectable half way measure between the booth and the formal dining room. Parents or grandparents might not be as enthused to have to swing a leg and pivot on a bench-style seat, so having the option of both works well. I believe having a playful type of seating is good for children. Getting them involved and excited to be at the table is important. Children who regularly attend meals as part of a structured family routine tend to have reduced rates of obesity and to eat more nutritiously. If you have the space, why not have both? A formal and informal eating area.

Family dynamics

Open-plan living gives you more awareness of what's going on in the home.

Do you love to be in control? Some say that being in control is a negative trait. Being in control may be a grey area for you, but for me it's black and white. With more control, I can make better decisions. Open plan gives you the opportunity to control how you feel, cook, entertain, and interact with your children, partner and friends. Control is great because it gives you that sense of consistency, commonality and order.

Being a parent is tough but rewarding. On the one hand, you need to care for and nurture your children, but on the other you have to be true to who you are. The ability to teach, to pass on wisdom and experience from our own lives, is awesome. It is said that if you want to know how much you know about a subject, you should teach someone. Whether or not you're a stay-at-home parent, you'll probably find yourself feeling that you need to be three people at once – or, more importantly, in three places at once.

Open plan gives you that opportunity to be in three places at once, because the room is those three places and you can see and hear everything that goes on. You can prepare food while your children play, feed them and then get on with tidying up after lunch or dinner. If your kitchen is closed off, you can get so wrapped up in looking after the children that you forget to eat.

My client Linda had just such an issue. She has a wonderful little boy, Thomas, who was thirteen months old and was just starting to walk. Linda said she needed to create a space that allowed her to be everywhere at all times. She wanted to keep Thomas in sight and be able to hear his pitter-patters as he moved around the room.

Linda didn't have a wide enough room for an island, but I was able to create a peninsula. I put the hob in the peninsula, as paying attention when cooking is important. The hob faced the living space, which had a sofa and space for Thomas's toys. Linda chose a practical flooring, Karndean, which is easy to clean. A large rug designated the living area and gave Linda the flexibility to move the sofa around the room as she saw fit.

Linda was blown away by how much flexibility the open-plan layout gave her. She loves to bake, but before with her closed-off kitchen she couldn't afford to leave Thomas in another room or have him under her feet while she baked. Now he can be playing with his train set or reading a book and she can be adding the cream cheese topping to her signature carrot cake. Linda now has control over her independence and parenting.

Social interaction

The social element is a clear reason for open-plan living. Socialising is something we all do. There are currently two billion active Facebook users, and you can tweet, snap, insta or pin on social media twenty four seven. You might meet friends at the pub for a drink before heading home. Social activities play a big part in our lives.

The modern household has no set agenda for roles or tasks – we share the responsibilities. If you had the space so that when you came in from work you could cook with your partner, as a team, how would that make you feel? One of you might be the stronger cook, but the head chef needs a sous chef to help lead the line, creating a team that whips through any recipe in no time. Share in the triumph of delivering that home-cooked nutritious meal. Call me an old romantic, but why not?

Think of a Saturday afternoon spent baking with the children. You're setting them up with the skills and passion that they'll take with them into later life. What would you give to ensure your children were getting a break from their phones, tablets and TV to get messy, get involved, with clumps of dough stuck between their fingers as they mix the shortbread ingredients?

35

Ever have those moments when you feel you haven't seen your friends for a while, because life just keeps getting in the way? Wouldn't it be great if you could invite them over and work together, side by side, chatting like it was only yesterday you last met? Take it in turns to stir the bolognaise sauce while you prepare the fresh green salad. Nothing matters but that moment, that memory that you have just created to add to your collection. Our brains crave the dopamine that we get from pleasurable social experiences. Treat yourself. Give your brain that fix that it demands and deserves.

Open-plan living allows you to multi-task more. You're playing host to your friends for a dinner party, and your partner's working the room and topping up the glasses. You have it all under control in the kitchen, not missing one second of the conversation. Your partner glides back to the kitchen area, pulling the plates out of the warming drawer to help you dish out the wild mushrooms in garlic and rosemary sauce. Never again will hosting be an effort.

Your teenage children arrive home from school with a friend or two. After helping you put away the shopping, they perch on the bar stools as they chat about their day, telling you how the science teacher taught them a really cool experiment with methane gas. Placing a plate of oatmeal biscuits and glasses of milk on the worktop, you make yourself a cup of coffee while still in earshot, remembering the excitement you felt when you were their age. They settle down to their homework while you set about getting ready for tea.

When you have a kitchen in harmony, these dreams are yours for the taking.

Harmony – Task

Before moving on to the next step, take a moment now to think about the 'why' for your open-plan kitchen. Write down your dream for the harmony your new kitchen will bring to your home, family, friends and life. I have a free interactive tool on my website if you would like additional help with this.

So, now you know your 'why' – what you're working towards – we can start looking at the 'how'. Next, we'll look at organisation.

Organisation

An organised home can be a harmonious home. When writing music, you need to organise and orchestrate the instruments and make sure the notes appear in the right place at the right time – otherwise, the harmony is off. In the kitchen, finding the right place for everything will allow you to entertain, cook and enjoy being with your family, instead of searching for the whisk!

Storage

When I was growing up we had a battery drawer in our house. You may know it as the man drawer, the hoarder's drawer or the odds and sods drawer. It's basically home to everything that doesn't really have a proper home. Batteries, takeaway menus, matches, spare keys, maybe even a random Lego police officer. My challenge to you is to take the sword to this drawer. It must be killed off and never spoken of again. It has no use in your life. You may be wondering where all those items will go. My answer is, they will be stored away in a designated place.

The reason this drawer, or even a whole cupboard designated to un-homed items, must go is simple – it's clutter. No different from clutter on your work desk. Because these items don't have a home you'll never be able to find what you're looking for when you really need it. Do you really need a pizza takeaway menu from 2012?

If you don't have a battery drawer, you're going to enjoy this section. A trend that has been gaining momentum is the industrial look – a version of minimalism, with open shelving. Open shelving is a wonderful phenomenon that should be embraced. It acts as a guiding principle: no clutter here, please. Open shelving is the polar opposite of the battery drawer. You can't hide anything on open shelving. It can't be bursting at the seams. It can't hold an assortment of breakable items placed precariously on top of each other, like the final round in the World Jenga Championship, before it all comes crashing down.

You might have shelving like this in the utility room, but you're now planning an open-plan kitchen and living space. You won't have a door you can close to hide the mess. You'll have to keep it tidy if you want to benefit from it. If I ever have a client who says they want a space to be clutter-free, I suggest open shelving.

You may gasp just like they did. But it's simple – we try not to care what people think of us, but it's completely natural to do so. Have you ever been on a date and deliberately avoided coming back to your place because you haven't tidied up? The state of your place is probably the last thing on their mind, but for you it seems like the biggest shame in the world because of how they may judge you. With open shelving, I don't think you'll be judged for what you have on display.

Open shelving works so well because it can be conversation starter and less can be more. Personal items like photos work best on open shelving. My wife has thousands of photos in her phone – I dare say we all do. She likes to go through them and get them printed. Why do we take a picture? To re-live the memory. To remind us of how we looked and felt and the emotions we shared. I encourage you to get pictures printed out to display on your open shelving.

I call personal items knick-knacks – they're more than just ornaments. They're more personal – maybe pebbles from the beach on your honeymoon, a set of old weighing scales or a glass figurine. There's no rhyme or reason to the items. They don't have to relate – they can be from different parts of your life – but they will invariably have an incredible amount of meaning for you. These items are great for open shelving. More memories for you to enjoy when you're in your favourite room in the house.

Open shelves can be an extension of your character – or, if you wish, the character you wish to portray. Hiring an interior designer to dress your shelves to a desired look or feel is great, too. Ultimately, it comes down to how it makes you feel and how it resonates with you. Personal objects speak to us on an empathic level, but so can non-personal items. Art is a great example of this. Well-selected, well-placed items on your open shelving will create a homely look.

Keep it flowing

Have you ever moved house? Whether you're upsizing or downsizing, you might have had that overwhelming feeling of where on earth is everything going to go?

Do you have a system? Are you a zen master who knows where everything will go? Or is it random, ad hoc? If you're upsizing, you could be overwhelmed with the amount of space you will have, finding that a cupboard only has one pan in it or the slow cooker will go above the fridge because it rarely gets used. You probably have some blindingly obvious processes in place, like putting the cups above the kettle and the tea and coffee jars, or storing the oven trays next to the oven or underneath the oven unit. Washing-up gloves and dishwasher tablets go under the sink. Nothing groundbreaking here, I know.

My dad had his garage set up like an operating theatre. Everything had a place and it was easily identifiable. You may be like this yourself or have a family member who has that large board on the wall, with an outline for each tool like a crime scene from the TV. My dad had the entire spanner set in ascending numerical size, so he would know straight away which item was missing. When I was eight there was no way I was that meticulous about organising the tools, but the system was clear. When I had to change the tyre on my pushbike, at least I knew where the socket I had used had come from.

Having a home for every item in the kitchen will help, but you might not need to be quite as specific as my dad. I literally snorted tea through my nose when it dawned on me that I've turned into my father. In my top drawer under the hob, which is home to all my cooking utensils and knives, I have set out small pegs so that only the right utensil can fit in the right place. As Pablo Picasso said, good artists borrow and great artists steal. And what a great idea I have commandeered.

You probably separate all the forks, knives and spoons, but do you have your starter forks and dessert forks separated from your main forks? One of the main reasons for having one spot for every item is that you don't want to waste time looking for it. This isn't foolproof, by any means. If the fish knife isn't in the drawer, it could already be out or it might be in the dishwasher. I'm talking about those exhausting conversations when you have to call out to your partner, 'Have you seen the fish knife?'

They reply, 'Yes I put it away.'

'I can't see it. Where did you put it?'

'In the drawer.'

'It's not in the drawer.'

'In the drawer with the bowls. I wasn't sure where to put it so I put it there until you needed it.'

I've had this conversation about a watch or a favourite pair of jeans, but I've never had it about equipment in our kitchen. Remember, I am my father's son, and everything has a home in our kitchen. Not wasting time is the first benefit, and the second might be a drop in the divorce rate!

When I was working in restaurants, the work flow of the kitchen was tight and well structured. I don't mean that the service was always smooth, because we're all human and fallible, but when things go wrong you need to be able to rely on your systems. The systems and process will reduce disruption and help you get back on track.

The first system in a restaurant is about the food delivery – always through the back of the restaurant and never the front, whether that's at six o'clock in the morning or four in the afternoon. Next up, storage – meat in the outside walk-in fridge, pulses and tins in the dry stores. When your shift starts you begin with food preparation, slicing, dicing, rolling, de-boning, peeling. No one was king in the kitchen: we all mucked in. Then you have the service itself, *mise en place* – plating up the food and getting it to the pass at the front of the kitchen, the quickest route to the seating area. Once the customers had finished eating, the plates would be cleared and brought to the pot-wash section, at the back of the kitchen, to reduce the risk of returning waiters colliding with those taking dishes to diners. Once the pot-wash team had worked their magic they would return our pots, pans, trays and plates to our stations so that we could start the process all over again. This was our workflow.

If you're like me, you probably have no desire to have a separate door to the sink area for when you've finished eating. Remember, if it's an open-plan kitchen, there's probably no door anyway. Restaurants set it up like this for efficiency. They're running a business so they want systems in place that increase productivity and avoid accidents, while providing the best possible dining experience for the customer.

Workflow patterns

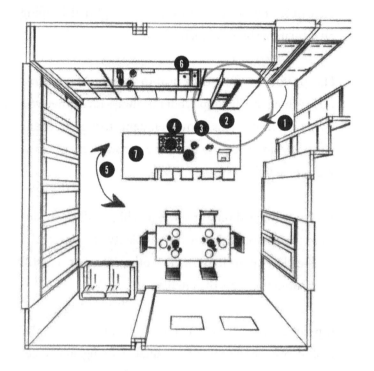

So what could workflow look like in your home?

1. Delivery of produce should come from the door/hallway with the easiest and most practical form of access to your kitchen.

2. Storing food should be as close as possible to your delivery access point. If achievable, having a fridge and dry stores/pantry in the same area.

3. Keeping the zone for all your knife work in the vicinity or edge of your food storage areas will be optimal, keeping all food items in easy reach.

4. Having your cooking zone next to your knife work area makes things really simple, but not always ideal when you have high level ovens. However, items that go in ovens generally don't require the same constant attention as items on a hob.

5. The route to the dining area will be a high traffic corridor so consideration to ensure there is plenty of room for the chef to plate up the food and that other kitchen users still have room to access the kitchen.

6. If practically possible, having a sink close to both the knife-work area and hob is invaluable. Being able to get both cold and boiling water quickly when recipes require it, for example boiling water for pasta or cold water for blanching vegetables. Not to mention keeping your work area clean and tidy as you work.

7. Having your crockery store close to your sink/dish-washer (6) and your plating up area/ route to the dining area (5) is also optimal.

From preparing toast with your morning coffee to full blown eight-course dinner parties, you will want the work flow of your kitchen to be smooth and effortless.

At Jacob Roberts we include this workflow pattern in kitchen designs for our customers. This makes sure you can be productive and creative in the kitchen area, without wasting time looking for the items you need. It makes the whole experience of cooking more satisfying and rewarding.

Kitchen practicals

Why is the kitchen island so important? It's an obsession for many, like the pot of gold at the end of the rainbow. You read newspaper articles, glossy home-improvement magazines, blog after blog, all shouting about the virtues of the kitchen island. This leads to high expectations about the island. So how has it commanded so much attention?

Maybe it's not your obsession, but it's certainly mine. Before I go to bed I'm checking websites and articles so see how the island can be improved. I think we can even take this discussion back to the fourth and fifth centuries. In ancient Greece, what we call the island was their table. The island's DNA was formed here. As the emperors lay around on benches, the servants (invariably slaves) would feed their masters. The masters would congregate and do business. I imagine this to be a room filled with raucous speech and music, the clinking of glasses, laughter, shouting and bartering.

My idea of the origin of the kitchen island surpasses the ancient Greeks. In fact, my theory takes us back to a time when there were no humans on the planet. I believe we can thank the animals and **edge effects** for the popularity of the kitchen island The edge effect is an ecological concept. Its principles describe how there is more diversity of life in the sweet spot where two opposite ecosystems overlap, such as land/water or forest/grassland.

Here's my take on it. Imagine the African Serengeti, home to grasslands and swamps. The grasslands are home to wild boar, antelopes and lions. The swamp is home to crocodiles and fish. The area of congregation for the mammals and reptiles is the land surrounding the watering hole. The mammals migrate to the water to hydrate, wash and cool off. The crocodiles venture out of the water to catch prey on the banks of the swamp and the open plain. You might think this is crazy, but stick with me here – are the chefs not our reptilian friends? In this analogy, the 'kitchen' side of the island is the lake and the 'living space' side of the island is the forest.

The kitchen side of the island is dangerous in our homes, too. Many sharp knives, and hot items like ovens and hobs. There's life and vitality in the shape of water from the tap and food in the cupboard and fridge. The living space side of the island, with the TV, sofa and dining table, where the children congregate, is like the grasslands. This is their environment. Think of your friends and family as the antelope who, whenever they are hungry, thirsty or intrigued, will make their way to the watering hole.

You may have a rogue antelope among your family or friends that ventures into the crocodiles' den to stir the tomato sauce or make a cup of tea, but most of your friends and family stay in the safety of the kitchen island – the banks of the swamp – to eat, drink and socialise.

A working island?

Back in the present day, the island offers security for guests, and a space for the chef to be creative and inspired. I really like working islands, which have a hob or a sink. If there isn't enough space for both, the chef in me always prefers to design a hob in the island rather than a sink. Like I said, cooking in front of guests is like being a DJ playing a gig, with the crowd in front of you full of anticipation and excitement. It's great theatre and adds to the occasion. More restaurants are opening up the kitchen to diners for this reason, allowing customers to be part of the experience.

I prefer not to put the sink in the island for three reasons:

1. Cooking is the main part of the evening, or at least a big part of the build-up. If your hob is on the outer perimeter of the island, the chances are that you'll either have your back to your guests or be side-on to them.

2. Depending on what sort of chef you are, you'll have all your *mise en place* ready or you'll be cooking on the fly. Either way, as you get on with the cooking, pans and trays and dishes will build up on the side. If you're having a party, the last thing you want is to be outshone by a stack of dirty dishes on the island. If the sink is in another part of the kitchen, that won't happen. Out of sight, out of mind.

3. I don't think we'll ever see restaurants installing viewing windows to the pot-wash area. I can't begin to tell you how valuable this area is to a well-functioning kitchen, but somehow I don't think people are interested in how the plates look after the meal. Call me daft, but I don't think it will catch on! It's the same in your home – guests aren't interested in watching you do the washing-up.

Organisation – Task

Ask yourself the following questions:

- Do you know where everything needs to be in your kitchen?

- How organised do you want to be?

- Do you want a working island? If yes, do you want one with a hob or with a sink?

Now you have thought through how you will organise your open-plan kitchen, we need to consider the mood you want to create.

Mood

The mood, or feeling, your open-plan kitchen creates depends on the lighting, what colours you use and what styles you choose. You can create an ambience that makes people feel welcome and happy, excited and enthusiastic or calm and chilled.

Lighting

If you spend longer than five seconds on social media, you're bound to come across a meme or two. They might make you smile or tip an imaginary cap to the wit. I like my quotes to have a little more substance.

'It is in our darkest moment that we must focus to see the light' – Aristotle.

I haven't included this quote to be cute. I believe that our greatest success comes from facing our fears head on, so this quote means a lot to me. We need light to see, of course, but it also affects how we feel.

Imagine you're in a proper old pub, with a thatched roof, low ceiling, exposed beams and a copper bar. It's autumn, and you step inside out of the crisp November air. You hear the roar of the fire, see the flicker of the flames as they dance in the fireplace. A solemn candle sways on each table. All you need now is a pint of the landlord's finest or a glass of wine. I'm there – I feel relaxed and chilled just thinking about it.

I don't know about you, but while I was daydreaming about that glass of wine, the roaring fire and dim light, the last thing on my mind was 'Let's get out my rolling pin and start preparing some shortcrust pastry cases'. The light in a room plays a huge part about how we feel in a situation. If you went to the cinema and they left the lights up, you probably wouldn't enjoy the film as much. Lighting affects the atmosphere of the room, and the atmosphere always plays a part in the experience.

People often tell me that they don't like their current kitchen because of the general lighting or ambient lighting. This could come from windows, doors and skylights, or chandeliers, table lamps and floor lamps. Small or ill-proportioned windows for the room will leave you feeling dissatisfied.

If you don't have enough light in a room to move around safely and perform simple tasks, think about adding more **general lighting**. You could add a window, with the obvious compromise of losing space for wall cupboards, or you might knock out a wall to benefit from the natural light in the other room. You might consider adding **task lighting** for cooking, reading or doing the paperwork. Task lighting should ensure an area is well lit – you don't want to get eyestrain, but you don't want glare from the lamp and it shouldn't cast any shadows.

In a gallery, the lamps hanging over the pictures and paintings are called **accent lighting**. These lamps guide you to focus on something interesting. If you have a vaulted ceiling or a double-height room, accent lighting will draw your eye up so you acknowledge the impressive ceiling heights. To make the most of accent lighting, it should be two and a half to three times brighter than the general lighting in the room.

Getting in the mood

How does using light change the way we feel? I call this **ambient** or **mood lighting**. My wife likes to tease me by saying that we could land a plane if we took the roof off our house because of the number of lights we have in our kitchen living space. We have six different lighting circuits in this space alone, which gives us the luxury of getting the mood just right for any occasion.

My favourite lights are the LED uplights. They sit in a concealed box section around the perimeter of the room and create a halo of light. As I sit here typing, I have a set of four spotlights over the sofa so I can see my laptop without squinting. I also have the under-cabinet lights on in the kitchen to illuminate this space. I feel relaxed, with an ample but not overpowering amount of light to work by.

You may feel this is overkill, and you could simply have some under-cabinet lights on and a floor lamp over where you were working. We chose to go to town on the lighting because we use the room for many different purposes and we wanted to be able to cover as many circumstances as possible. If you have a large open-plan room, you might not be able to have floor lamps without running cables across walkways. If you choose to have floor-mounted sockets under sofas or chairs, you might have to keep the furniture in the same positions.

Our brief from Mr Duke was to build a space that all three members of the family could enjoy together. The Smiths love cooking together and wanted to display their cookery books and try new cooking methods. It was important to the family

that their room felt light and bright, so we added lighting above the oven units to give the impression of more height and to use as ambient lighting. The ceiling height was a great feature in the dining area, so we included some light boxes to illuminate the ceiling and draw the eye upwards. The family also wanted a visual feature as you walk into the room, so we incorporated a lit display area, which could be left open or used to display items that are important to them.

However you choose to incorporate lighting into your home, mood lighting is that balance that adds *feeling* to a room. A simple dimmer switch might be your chosen solution. Mood lighting sits between task and accent lighting. You have enough light to make a cup of tea, but not too much to distract you from that latest episode on catch-up. Just like at the cinema during the trailers.

Structural glass

Nine out of ten new clients I visit explain that they're thinking about a new extension and they want it to be an open-plan kitchen with bi-folding doors. Bi-folding doors are usually floor-to-ceiling glass panels that you can fold back to open up the whole wall. The technology is improving all the time, and they give a room that much-needed injection of natural light and a feeling of space. These large expanses of glass are a way of bringing the outside in, and create the feeling that the inside merges with the outside.

Sliding doors are great too. They can be fitted as one casement that passes by either a fixed pane or another sliding door. They don't have as many vertical frame lines as bi-folding doors do. Each bi-folding door needs its own frame so it can fold into a concertina when it is fully open. Sliding doors are like massive picture frames to capture the views, whether that's your garden or the rolling hills beyond. Sliding doors don't create as open a feeling as bi-folding doors do. When bi-folding doors are fully open, they are folded to one side. Sliding doors only ever open as far as the pane of glass allows, so you don't get that fully open feel.

Pocket doors are an exception to the rule, because they slide into the wall. This means, for example, that if you had an opening of six metres for sliding doors you would need a wall length of three metres either side of that opening. This gives the pocket doors somewhere to hide when they're fully open.

Structural glass jobs capture my attention. I love using frames and panes of glass to make walls of expansive light that flood into a building. Or designing two storeys of floor-to-ceiling fixed glass, building mezzanine floors to create a truly open-plan home. Even the upstairs gets to be part of the downstairs. It's unlikely that you would build something like this for an urban, semi-detached property, but it highlights how you can use glass and light in practical ways to make even the tiniest of spaces more usable.

Colour

To write about colour and trends is a challenge, as what I write now could be outdated in just a few years. If you bought this book around 2018, I hope you find this section helpful and insightful. If your robot butler has downloaded it from the main server in 3018, I hope you have a few chuckles.

If you want to predict what styles will be bang on trend, look at the catwalk. The catwalk makes waves and we ride the surf to shore. Of course, not all catwalk colours translate well into the home, but the biggest trends do so eventually. Manufacturers have to bear the brunt of the development costs. Five years ago you couldn't avoid hearing, seeing and reading about white gloss kitchens. White with black worktops was super trendy, and this monochrome look was a staple for years. I wasn't a fan, but my reasons were biased – 'Oh, what a nice change to be fitting another white and black kitchen!'

At the time of writing, the real mover and shaker is grey (thankfully, not fifty shades). Grey is certainly proving to be the new black. While I'm not governed by colour trends, I do follow what other manufacturers are doing. When you move from finding just one grey in the shops to seeing ten different shades in matt and gloss finishes, it certainly speaks volumes.

The greys that may be taking your fancy right now are likely to be dove grey, French grey, stone grey or graphite. These are not industry standards – one manufacturer's French grey may be another's stone grey – so you won't always be comparing like with like.

This is not the case when the colour is a natural colour system (NCS) colour. Each NCS colour has a unique code to ensure that it is exactly the same every time it is replicated.

Colours are also linked to where you live. People in rural areas are likely to be more conservative with colour. In large cities with diverse cultures and tastes, people are going to flaunt more variety, daring and eccentricity.

I call it yellow briefcase syndrome. If you meet ten accountants from the same sized firm, with the same credentials and the same ability to serve your needs, you'll remember the one who arrived with a yellow briefcase. I love that people are pushing the boundaries of personalisation, looking to stand out and celebrate being different. If you want a jet-black kitchen or a fluorescent pink kitchen, why the flip not? If that's what's makes you happy, do it!

Having said that, only those who have owned a high-gloss black kitchen will understand the perils. High gloss looks stunning and it keeps you honest – there's nowhere to hide. It shows everything. The way it catches the light makes fingerprints as obvious and eye-catching as a neon light outside a nightclub. High-gloss black looks its best on the day it's handed over. Unused, untouched and not even breathed on.

Don't be scared – if you like black, there is a solution. If this is indeed the year 3018 I hope a material has been invented that doesn't allow fingerprints and other marks to be left on doors. Failing that, if black is your preferred colour, a matt finish works well, especially in a hand-painted kitchen. It doesn't catch the light anywhere near as much as gloss does. It's far more forgiving with fingerprints and if you have children or pets, matt will be fine with these too.

Trendy?

So how did black and white dominate the kitchen trend for so long? They complement each other, like any great couple, partnership or marriage. A black yin to the white yang. Black is the absorption of all colours. It represents, power, control, discipline and authority. We may even associate it with sexiness – the slender and sleek little black dress. White represents innocence and wholeness. Traditionally, brides wear white to symbolise that they are ready for the new beginning that is their marriage. Too much white can appear sterile, though, like a doctor's jacket, and white can be cold and lacking in emotion.

While there is no denying that grey is gunning for the number one spot, it needs a partner to share the glory. Grey and grey don't make a power couple, certainly not one that rivals monochrome. I dare say that black and white will make a comeback in the next twenty-five years.

Another celebrity couple to arrive on the scene in the last five years was cream and green (or willow, thyme or sage). It was only big for a while, but it hasn't faded out completely.

A common concern when designing a new kitchen is to avoid choosing a colour scheme that will date too quickly. Name one thing that hasn't dated. You haven't even had your new phone for two months before there are updates to the apps. Your car was once a horse and cart, and we are now speeding into a world of driverless cars. We can't avoid the evolution that leads to what was once new becoming outdated.

When it comes to colour, if you're afraid that your kitchen will look outdated, go with black and white. It worked then, it works now and it will work twenty-five years from now. I don't think it's the colour you're worried about, it's the value of your home. Your real concern is, 'If I sell my house in X years, will it be desirable to a big enough market?'

With the housing shortage we have in the UK, I can't imagine that the colour of your kitchen will stop you selling your home – even if you went for a day-glow yellow and red kitchen. I strongly believe you should go for what makes you happy. Choose a powerful combination of two colours you like – colours that speak to you and have meaning to you – and dive in. I would much rather have a couple of years of absolute bliss and enjoyment from my kitchen than settle for playing it safe live on the off chance that I might sell my house more easily.

Door styles

There are four main types of doors: slab, shaker, handleless and in-frame. Then you have a multitude of finishes within these ranges.

A slab door is a plain door, with little or no detail on it. The core of the door can differ from manufacturer to manufacturer, but the two most common ones are MDF or chipboard. If the front is laminated (with a plain colour, a wood texture or wood grain), the base will probably be chipboard. The difference between the two is negligible. Chipboard and MDF reduce the likelihood of the door twisting. Real wood expands and contracts as the temperature in your home changes.

Vinyl doors are very popular, and new colours are always being added to keep up with trends and fashions. To make a vinyl door, a thin material is glued to the core of the door. When you're looking at doors in a showroom, if you can see a hairline around the rear face of the door it will be a vinyl door. Poor-quality vinyl doors may 'orange peel' – when a door catches the light, it looks like the skin of an orange. This is caused by the bonding process and the quality of the vinyl. Vinyl offers you the widest variety of colours, in gloss and matt finishes.

For a small difference in cost, which could be as little as couple of pounds, acrylic doors are a fabulous alternative to vinyl. Most acrylic doors are edged with PVC and then laser cut. The finishing process is clean and this creates a better door.

For the full glossy effect, you might want to consider a lacquered door. These sprayed doors have a finish like mirrors and they look fantastic. They catch the light and can make a dull room much brighter.

Matt finishes are now starting to stamp their authority. If you've chosen one of the 1,970 NCS colours to put a truly personal stamp on your kitchen, you'll need to choose the finish. You could have a structured or silk lacquered finish. The silk finish is smooth and soft to the touch. The structured lacquer has a texture to it, like fine sandpaper, raised and stippled under the fingertips.

Shaker-style doors are classic. They have survived the test of time and probably will continue to do so. A traditional shaker door is made from five pieces of wood – one simple flat panel and four pieces to make the raised frame. These doors are assembled using the tongue-and-groove technique. Some manufacturers have developed a way of making a shaker door from a single piece using special machinery. This one piece shaker door is a modern take on a traditional door and we have seen its popularity grow.

Handleless doors. Sleek and seamless straight lines have become more popular in kitchen design, and this look is achieved by using handleless doors. The most common rebuff to the handleless door is fingerprints. But in almost all cases you put your fingertips behind the door to pull it open or into a small groove. You can find out more about these options and how to create this slim, sleek look in the handleless section.

In-frame kitchen doors are beautiful. In-frame doors are made to fit inside the carcass of the wooden unit, which makes them a more costly option, but they're worth the investment if that's the style you want for your dream kitchen. Traditional in-frame doors have a little butt hinge and a magnetic catch. You can have a soft-close in-frame door, but for me there's something romantic about the little click as the magnetic catch pulls the door closed.

A splatter, a splash and a drip

So what do you do with the gap between the worktop and the bottom of the wall units? Do you need to do anything at all? What are the benefits of getting it covered? Would a durable paint finish be enough? Let's break it down and see what our findings are. The reason you need to cover this part of the walls is obvious – you want to protect the areas that are most likely to be affected by water, grease or food spills. The two most important areas are likely to be around the sink and the hob, unless you have your hob in the island or peninsula.

Before we cover materials, here is my view. When planning your kitchen, decide which part has to speak volumes to you – the bit of the kitchen you want to show off. If you're planning to use neutral colours for the main parts of the kitchen, like whites, creams and greys, you might want to use accenting to build colour into your space. Accenting components can be easily changed to bring a new lease of life to a tired kitchen.

If you want to complement your units with something bold, striking or even playful, it's about finding a balance. Having cabinet doors with a high level of detail and then adding stimulating, loud tiling is like wearing polka-dot shorts and a Hawaiian shirt. Each to their own, but that's a lot of colour and stimulation going on even for the most confident fashionista. In the right setting they can hold their own, but not when displayed together.

The easiest way to achieve a subtle and clean finish is an upstand. An upstand is a continuation of the worktop that rises above the worktop by 100mm. It's usually 20mm thick. Then, you can paint the wall between the top of the upstand

and the bottom of the wall units. Upstands work well around sink areas too. I like to see the worktops, windowsills and upstands all in the same material, especially if it's granite or quartz.

The only caveat I place on upstands is the area around the hob. You'll probably add a different material behind the hob if the hob is placed against a wall. It may be something as simple as a sheet of stainless steel, or it could be some tiles or a glass splashback. You can use the same material as the upstands to make the splashback behind the hob, but only if the design can take it.

Tiles are your go-to option if you don't fancy upstands. Colours and sizes will float in and out of fashion, but what looks set to stay are the brick-effect metro tiles. These 200mm by 100mm tiles look effective and can be spiced up with a contrasting grout. At a smidge over 40 pence per tile, you could have a really cost-effective finish to your kitchen. The main bugbear with tiles is that the grout can start to look dirty and grubby in a short time. One overexuberant stir of tomato soup or bolognaise and your white gloss tiling could remind you of it for years to come. Even if you were the most diligent of cleaners you could miss one or two tiny splatter marks.

On the other hand, tiling can hide a multitude of sins, including imperfections in the wall and plastering. I don't recommend this, but I have seen examples of tiling over existing tiles. The irony of tiling is that if you're removing tiles you hope they've been poorly fitted and just pop off the wall, but if you're having them fitted you hope they've been professionally installed. When tiles need to be taken off they can leave quite a mess, taking the plaster with them because they were so well bonded to it.

Next on the hot list is glass. Back-painted glass splashbacks are growing in popularity. They're more costly to install than tiles, but there are some advantages to using glass. Glass splashbacks are super-easy to keep clean – warm soapy water on a damp cloth is all you need, and you can buff them with a microfibre cloth. You can easily get sheets of glass in 2.4 metre lengths, so the joints between them are usually in the corners or between walls.

The process of getting glass splashbacks is time-consuming – even the most efficient of manufacturers take around two weeks. A template for the glass has to be made after the worktops have been installed. Templating is normally carried out to a tolerance of about 2mm, which may sound a lot but in real numbers it is tiny. Your home will expand and contract and if the glass is fitted tight it could shatter. Once the glass has been cut to size and the holes for the sockets have been cut out of it, it is toughened. Toughened glass smashes into a million pieces if you chip or break it. Once a piece has been toughened it cannot be altered, so if it's the wrong size or shape you'll need to have a new piece made.

Get a grip on handle styles

Handles are an important part of the kitchen, not just because you need them to open the doors. You could have a traditional pull handle, with a wide range of choices and styles. You might prefer the handleless style, with J-groove, rebated doors or a handle groove built into the units. You also have the push-catch system (when you push the door to open it) and the servo-driven systems which can be wired up to work from sensors that detect movement. All these options have pros and cons, some bigger than others.

Why are handles so important? Because they're a reflection of style, like an awesome pair of shoes, a statement necklace or a beautiful watch that completes your outfit. You can be daring, adventurous, playful or eclectic with your choice of handles. In contrast, a handleless system doesn't mean you're any less playful, adventurous or daring – it just says you have a different design focus. About 65% of my clients moved away from traditional handles for the simple reason that they caught on clothes and pockets. If you've ever owned a knitted jumper, you'll know what it's like to be walking away from the kitchen only to be dragging a drawer or door with you. If you like eclectic or unusual handles, then telling you this is unlikely to change your decision. The practicalities are going to be outweighed by its aesthetics.

Traditional pull handles are popular. You can pay anything from a few pounds to hundreds of pounds – you can even walk into a reclaim yard and pick up ten handles for a fiver. Price and weight are usually good indications of quality. For example, two different T-bar handles of similar length could feel noticeably different. The better quality handle would weigh more because a higher quality of metal has been used. Of course, black carbon-fibre handles to match your Ferrari-red kitchen will weigh next to nothing and will still cost you a small fortune. In general, different grades of metal are used for handles and the cost is usually reflected accordingly.

If you prefer handleless doors, J-groove handles work well because this won't affect the sizes of the units. There are some slight restrictions with J-groove handles in vinyl doors, because nasty creases can form when the vinyl cannot fold properly. Some manufacturers overcome this by making the depth of the J-groove shallower. The second limitation is with built-in appliances. In some manufacturers' fitting instructions, the fixings for the appliance go through the thinnest part of the door. Check with your designer or installer when choosing your door and appliances to get advice. J-groove doors work well if they are sprayed and lacquered, because then there are no unsightly creases. Not all manufacturers can offer a full colour range in J-groove designs, so be careful to check whether you can get the colour you want.

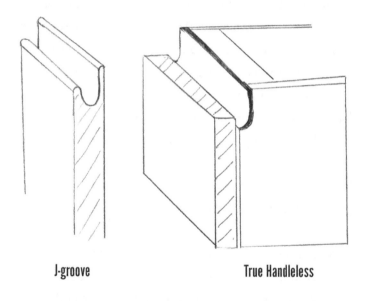

J-groove   True Handleless

The in-built handle system works well too. European kitchens have been built in this way for many years, so it's a tried-and-tested system. Today, there are better materials and finishes, with fewer laminates and more stainless-steel trims. Manufacturers used laminates to match the handle to the finish of the door, or provide a contrast with the brushed stainless-steel look. Keller are able to match all the 1,970 NCS colours used for door finishes with a metal track system. This system is practical because there is nowhere for crumbs to collect, unlike the J-groove system, which can become a food trap.

The fundamental difference to the J groove and the built-in (also known as true handless) is the handle trim system. As you can see from the profile on the J groove door, the door is machined into a J and you hook finger tips over the leading edge of the door to pull it open. With the built-in track the handle rail is machined into the unit not the door. Aesthetically, both systems appear seamless. In some designs it is nice to contrast the rail with a different colour to the door, but this is not as common with the J groove because of the manufacturing process involved.

There's a time and place for push-catches. I think they solve a problem that wasn't there to start with. As a fitter I didn't like them, because for the catches to work efficiently they needed to be positioned slightly off the unit to give the catch enough room to disengage and let the door spring forward when you push it. You're still going to need a handle for any integrated appliances you have, and whether you choose a fixed handle or handle track, the seamless look will be compromised. Maybe I'm being too judgemental, but I can think of many better ways to achieve a seamless, sleek look and leave the push-catches in the box where they belong.

Mood – Task

Think about the mood you want to create in your kitchen.

Decide which mood you want to create in your dream kitchen by choosing from the following words (or adding your own):

relaxed	exciting	calm	modern
comforting	energetic	romantic	futuristic
homely	welcoming	young	chilled
tranquil			

Equipment

You can't create a great symphony without the right instruments. Your dream kitchen needs the right combination of

73

equipment. Now we're going to look at how to make sure your units are up to the job, the heating is right, the worktops are suitable, you have the appropriate appliances and you can manage those delightful cooking smells.

Units

My favourite film is *The Blind Side* with Sandra Bullock. It's based on the true story of a young man who is taken in by a kind and caring family who nurture his natural talent for American football. My own blind side came when I left my employer of eight years to set up on my own. I didn't know what I didn't know, especially when it came to kitchen units. As a professional in the industry, the choice in the market can be overwhelming. What are the differences? How do you choose between them? Do you use price as a yardstick? What is a high-quality unit? What's not a high-quality unit?

The units are important because they are your foundation. You want these to last. I had only ever used one manufacturer when I was employed, but it gave me a great understanding. The units I used back then were fitted on large commercial sites in London. They were 18mm thick with solid backs. But they were flat-pack. Plenty of people think flat-pack units are bad, but I will explain why they're not:

- ACCESS. Access to the building or kitchen is often limited. You can carry and manhandle flat-pack boxes of kitchen units far more efficiently than a cumbersome fully-assembled unit.

- ALTERATIONS. To make a quick alteration to flat-pack units is simple – you undo the cams (cams are what lock the panels together) and you can remove or alter the back or side panels easily.

When a unit is rigid (already assembled) it might have been glued together or held together with wooden dowels. Sometimes the unit is assembled but not glued, which saves money because you don't have to pay your tradesperson to build the units.

Which is best, flat-pack or rigid? Some retailers will tell you their units come rigid and this makes them a better quality. But that's like saying, 'We have fitted the baby seat in that new car you bought'. The action of fitting the car seat is irrelevant if the baby seat is not up to the approved safety standards.

18mm or 16mm?

What does quality look like? There are some fantastic UK manufacturers out there who will produce an 18mm carcass all round. This means tops, bottoms, sides and back. They are great. Heavy, but great.

Some manufacturers make 16mm carcasses to save money, as 16mm board is cheaper. At the volume these manufacturers are producing, cost is important to their low price business model.

The problem with units that are 18mm all round is that they are heavy. This is fine for a base unit, because the floor is taking the weight and load. When it comes to wall units, the extra weight poses a few more problems. The hanging brackets are only designed to carry a certain weight. A dinner set for eight, with eight main plates, side plates, bowls and cups, can weigh 4.5 kilograms. Rarely do you only have eight cups, and I'm fairly confident that you have at least few more place settings. If you have an 18mm unit, most of the capacity of the hanging brackets is taken up with the weight of the unit, before you even put in your crockery. Kitchens with large drawers to hold your crockery are better suited to handle this, but if you don't have the space, you'll still put your plates, bowls and cups in the wall units.

The problem is even bigger when you have extra-tall wall units. Probably, the hanging brackets will be the same but the cupboard will be heavier, so you can't put as much in the units. Another thing to consider is the type of wall you are hanging the cupboards on. A solid brick wall offers more support than a stud wall. If the wall is ply lined, or battened out to where the wall hanging brackets will affix to, that will certainly help. In newer properties, there is often only one skin of plasterboard. To overcome this problem, ask the installer or designer to use load-spreading hanging brackets.

In Europe it's common for manufacturers to use 16mm carcasses with hardboard backs, which could be conflicting; as I mentioned, 16mm is used as a cost saving measure. Consider whether you would prefer an 18mm panel made out of Weetabix or a 16mm panel made of titanium. The thickness isn't what determines the quality of the unit – its quality is defined by its properties and density. A high quality 16mm panel used in the construction of a unit will outperform an 18mm in key areas.

The backs of the units were a stumbling block for me. I always thought a thicker back was important. The most important purpose of the back is to stop the unit twisting. A thicker back, cut to the correct dimensions and fitted tightly between the side panels, doesn't allow the unit to twist and be 'out of square' (not set to 90 degrees). But the 18mm backs are heavier.

If you've ever assembled flat-pack furniture, you'll have seen that thin (4–6mm) backs sit in a rebate. This pocket is oversized to allow you to slide the back panel in easily. This keeps the weight down but allows the unit to twist like a trapezium. How do the Europeans get round this? They use lasers in the manufacturing process. When the units come down the production line, the production worker has laser markers to make sure the units are square before they are assembled and glued. This is how they counter the weight and construction issues that other manufacturers face.

Cooking smells

I trawl the internet for chat rooms where people are discussing kitchens and open-plan design to better understand what problems customers have and to find solutions. Kitchen smells come up regularly.

I love to cook fajitas. They're quick and easy, and they align with our family philosophy of 'put it together yourself' cooking. The chef in me gets the pan glowing – I want this crispy veg to fry, not stew. By the time I've added the oil and spice it's about to get real. The kitchen starts to smell. With some food you will never completely get rid of the smell. Do you need an extractor?

One of the biggest problems with extractors is that you need to get the smell out of the house. Two things affect this: how big the room is and how far the air has to travel before it is expelled into the open. When you're looking for an extractor, you will be shown a number that looks like this: xxx m³/h. This is the cubic volume of air that the extractor moves in one hour. There are a few really powerful domestic extractors on the market that can boast numbers over 750m³/h. Several manufacturers use a motor this big. Blanco, the German manufacturer is one. These styles of extractor are known as canopy extractors and are fitted into a mantle-style kitchen (common with in-frame or shaker-style kitchens) or in decorative units, normally the same colour as the doors.

There are two restrictions when fitting an extractor:

1. WHERE THE KITCHEN IS. If you live in a semi-detached or terraced house and the kitchen is located on the adjoining wall, you won't be able to extract air into your neighbour's home. If the kitchen is on an exposed brick wall and that wall is a boundary wall, some planning

offices will not allow you to extract air directly into the neighbour's garden.

You need to check that the joists run in your favour if you want to extract the air through another wall. If the joists do not run parallel to the direction you want to run your extractor vent, this will cause you problems. You don't want to drill 100mm diameter holes in every one of your joists for the ductwork, because it will weaken your joists. In newly built homes you can choose to have webbed joists that have specific service holes for pipe-work and electrical wiring. Unfortunately, your 1970s home will not have been fitted with these favourable joists.

There are solutions. If the hob is fitted on the outer perimeter of the kitchen on a back wall, you can hide the duct behind fly-over panels and a cornice. Thin 50mm ductwork is fitted on top of the units and connected to a brick-effect grille vented outside.

2. WHERE THE OVEN AND HOB ARE. What if you have a working island with a hob and the joists don't run parallel to the direction you want to expel the air? You can use a charcoal filter. It's never going to work as well as a filter that extracts air outside, but it is better than nothing. Every bend in the ductwork reduces the efficiency by 50%.

If the duct is too long or there are too many bends for the extractor unit, you might need a helping hand from sub-extractors along the way. This isn't a problem for a charcoal filter. These filters need replacing so they can cope with the demands of cooking. Yearly is fine. Usually all you have to do is take out a single screw or pull catch to replace the filter.

Martin wanted to protect his child from airborne pollutants. Asthma affects 67 in 100 children in the UK, and Martin's son had a severe case. Martin bought every air purifier he could get, constantly looking for the newest design to help make his son's life more comfortable. It took him four years, but the results are remarkable. He has produced a machine that can eliminate food odours and gets rid of pollen and bacteria – it produces 95% clean air.

Martin's invention was PlasmaMade. It's a plasma filter that attaches to your extractor and removes the need for any ductwork out of the house. What is great is that there is a company that produces pendant light shades with built-in extractors that are attached to the plasma filter. This means we can now design functional art that acts to remove our cooking smells. As most people like to have pendant lights above the kitchen island, it's a fantastic solution to the problem of getting rid of those unwanted smells.

Heating

How do you heat open-plan spaces? We are bombarded with ways to save energy and reduce bills – save this, switch now, gas is on the rise, increases in electricity prices. We can, and should, be diligent in how we manage our consumption. If you've installed solar panels on your home, I tip my cap to you. How nice it must be to get a cheque from your utility provider. Have you seen the waves Elon Musk and Tesla are making with their solar panel roof tiles? Inspirational.

Have you ever stayed in a luxury hotel with underfloor heating? The feeling of underfloor heating is bliss. It's not just cosy, but comforting to the touch. If you're anything like me, if your feet are warm, so are you. As soon as my feet get cold, my whole body feels cold. Think of your feet as a car radiator. The radiator has lots of fins or tubes (the zig-zag bits of metal). The larger the surface area of fins, the larger the volume of air being forced through to cool the water down. Our feet work in a similar way. The foot has many veins that run close to the surface. We do not have as many muscles in our feet, so we don't store as much heat and we can lose the heat more easily when we stick our feet out of the bed to cool down.

There are two types of underfloor heating: electrical matting and water-pipe systems. Both have merits. Although electrical matting is more expensive to run, it is cheaper to install. The water-pipe system is cheaper to run but more expensive to install. If you have it hooked up to solar panels, the sun's rays top up the heat of the water. As the pump pushes the water round the pipes, the temperature is regulated efficiently. In fact, that's one of the reasons underfloor heating is popular. It heats the concrete and screed floor that covers it, and the floor gives off the heat slowly and constantly throughout the day. You won't get that instant gratification that you would if you lit a fire or put on the central heating, but for a steady room temperature, underfloor heating works well.

The electrical matting works well too. A great benefit of this matting is that it doesn't raise the floor as dramatically as water-pipe underfloor heating does, so it can be retro-fitted to one room. The pipe version could end up raising the floor by as much as 60mm, the same as three fingers. The alternative is to dig the floor out to gain the depth you want, but this is not always possible or practical. It depends on what kind of foundations your home has.

Heat-recovery systems. Heat goes up, which is why your mum and dad made you wear a hat in the snow – we lose a lot of heat from our heads. That's also why heat-recovery systems are great. If you dream of building your own home, or you're in the process of doing it, consider a passive house – a Scandinavian-style flat-pack house with panels that get delivered and put up quickly and are highly insulated. Heat-recovery units collect the heat that has risen from ground level. The heat is then stored and used to top up the water system that runs through a pipe at ground level.

Radiators work really well too. Check the output you need for the space you are trying to heat. The output is given in British thermal units (BTUs). There's a video on my website that explains how to work out BTUs and what size radiator you will need. One main thing to consider with a large area is that you may need a few small radiators rather than one large one, because even a large radiator may not provide enough output to heat the space.

How many radiators you can fit in the room will depend on how much wall space you have. In an open-plan set-up, you aren't likely to have as much wall space. Tall designer or vertical radiators work well in this situation. They act as a statement piece for the room while making the most of a narrow but full-height bit of wall. The colour and styles on the market right now can be easily considered as art. It might not be a Rembrandt, but in my humble opinion a well-crafted, well-designed radiator can certainly add to the story of the room.

Worktops

Increased worktop space is a must in any kitchen design. It should cover a larger footprint than the floor area in that workflow space. What kind of worktop should you choose? We all want different things from our worktops. Budget is a big part of planning what to do with your kitchen.

Granite is really expensive, right? Well, not really. Granite has become more and more popular, and that means there are more installers and even more suppliers to feed the demand. In plain English, prices have been getting cheaper every year. If your gorgeous new worktops were going to cost £3,500, is that a sizeable chunk of money? You wouldn't be crazy for wanting to get at least ten years' use out of your kitchen. If you used your kitchen morning and evening, six days a week, for 48 weeks of the year, over five years every time you used the kitchen it would cost you £1.20 to have these beautiful worktops. That's less than the cost of a cup of coffee.

Let's take a look at the options.

Laminates are your most cost-effective solution. There are hundreds of colours and styles to choose from, and many manufacturers. With advances in technology, there are now some laminates on the market that you can have with an under-mounted sink. You can't have drainer grooves shaped into the worktops, because the laminate isn't deep enough to get the fall needed for the water to run off into the bowl.

Laminates should always be mason-mitred. This process of cutting a male and female section makes the joint appear seamless when butted together. There is no real excuse for using those metal strips that you can buy from hardware stores. They collect all sorts of dirt, grime and food debris which is how they later gained the name salmonella strips. Laminates should be cut using a router and then sealed with silicone or wood glue. I prefer silicone because of its barrier to water. You can buy coloured sealants, but any kitchen fitter who is worth their salt won't need to use that because they can get the joint so clean and tight.

White laminate worktops are the hardest to join because the laminate has a dark backing. If the job is done poorly you'll see the faint black line on the joint. Black worktops are the easiest, and they're more forgiving for the same reasons as above.

Please do not go for a cheap laminate. Always look for the drip strip. You can find the drip strip underneath the worktop, set back 15–20mm. The drip strip is included because if you ever spill water or splash it excessively around the sink, the water runs off the worktop, gets as far as the drip strip and then falls to the floor. If a worktop doesn't have a drip strip, the water seeps in where the laminate meets the chipboard or backing paper and is absorbed. Over time, this builds up and rots the chipboard or blows the laminate.

Real wood. A fantastic example of real wood worktops is the butcher block, where different coloured lengths of wood are glued together. The staves could be of the same type – for example, oak, walnut, cherry or beech – but the varied tones and colours give the worktop a beautiful natural look.

Real wood is great for kitchens with a curved or abstract design, because you can template and shape the worktops however you want. Real wood can be glued together to make the worktops wider than standard laminates, which come in 600mm, 670mm and 900mm widths. That's why laminate breakfast bars are 900mm wide. With wood, you can easily join it, add a tight radius or create smooth concave corners.

Wood does need some tender love and care. You will want to oil it every six months to keep it looking as good as the day it was installed. If wood gets scratched or dented, you can sand it with an orbital sander. If the scratches are light, you could even sand them by hand. If you take a hot pan off the hob or a tray out of the oven and put it straight onto the wood, it will probably mark or burn the worktops. You could sand them, but whether this will work depends how deep the burn mark goes. It could go up to 6mm deep, which is a long way to go to sand it out. It's best to have a protective mat or metal rack to hand or some heat bars built into the worktops. I really like to mix wood with granite or quartz surfaces, because it adds warmth, texture and an organic element to the design.

Concrete worktops. If you're on Pinterest, I'd be amazed if you haven't come across a tutorial on how to make concrete worktops on your feed. Although concrete is relatively cheap, making the mould is expensive. Basically, to make a concrete worktop you build upturned boxes and pour in the cement, strengthening it with iron bars or rods to help take the flex, and allow it to dry slowly so that it doesn't crack. That's fine if you just want a single slab. The difficulty comes when you want drainer grooves drop-end panels, sink and hob cut-outs, or a detail on the front edge. The real skill is in designing and building the mould.

Unlike wood, with concrete you can put a hot pan straight onto the worktop, which is handy. But concrete gets marked down for being porous. If you spill red wine or turmeric, you'll need to clean it up straight away so you don't stain the worktops. I really like concrete; it has an honest and authentic look and feel. It makes a statement but goes about it in a quiet and soft manner. If you're going for an exposed-brick industrial look then consider concrete worktops. You don't necessarily have to do the whole room in them – just the island, for example, would complement the design.

Quartz and granite. What are the differences between quartz and granite, and what does it mean to you? Granite and quartz have some fundamentally different properties. These won't necessarily change how you use your kitchen, but there are some practicalities to consider.

Granite is the natural stone that is excavated out of the ground from quarries and mountains. It is a fossil. Because it is a natural product, there will be slight differences between your worktops. Think of the large stone pieces as being like a loaf of bread. As you cut the bread into slices, how it looks will change slightly. You may get an air bubble in the loaf, and this is similar to the veins that you see in the worktops.

For the best result, ask your installer to book-match the worktops. Continuing with the bread analogy, to get the best match you would take two slices that are next to each other. They are similar in shape, size and appearance. When you do this with slabs of granite, it gives you a consistent look and colour throughout the kitchen. That being said, you may still get some slight variance from slab to slab. Your stone manufacturer should always try to book-match the tops, but you might need to pay a little more for this.

The downside of granite is that if you need to match it later on, it might not be possible. For example, if you have granite worktops fitted in the kitchen and then a few years later you decide you're going to do the utility room, you might not be able to buy the same stone that you had for the kitchen. It's likely to be from the same quarry and be the same colour, but it's almost never from the same block as the slabs you got for the kitchen.

You can put pans straight down onto granite, but I don't recommend it. If you can touch the pan with your hand, it is cool enough to place it on the surface. But if any moisture happened to be trapped in your worktop and you added the heat of a pan or tray, the moisture could expand and crack the granite.

On certain overhangs, or next to the sink or hob, you'd have to have iron rods added to your worktop. This is to strengthen it. Even when these brittle stone tops are being handled on site, they must be moved with the utmost care – otherwise, they could snap.

You can add some wonderful effects to granite. It can be honed to a matt finish, which looks stunning but will leave fingerprints. You can also have a flamed or a leather effect, which is like a stippled effect over the face of the worktop. This gives it an original, unique and authentic look. Granite is porous, so after the tops have been installed the fitter will put a sealer over them. This won't stop everything getting through, but you can consider it splash-proof.

Marble. White worktops are increasing in popularity, especially white with a dark veining. Typically the natural product that matches this description is marble. Marble looks great in a bathroom, but is simply too soft to use in a kitchen, so if you want natural white tops with the dark veins consider quartz.

Quartz worktops are made by setting quartz chippings in a resin. It is a man-made product, which means that the worktop colour, how sparkly it is, the size of the chippings and so on can all be precisely measured. These worktops are made in batches, so there could be slight differences from batch to batch, but on the whole this is unlikely.

Because the tops are a composite, they are far more suitable for overhangs, technical details and fragile weak points. They are non-porous, so they are more resistant to staining. With larger stone chippings, though, there is a chance that a stain could seep in between the chipping and a resin pocket. These pockets are tiny, but they could get discoloured. If you have a worktop with a fine crush or almost solid colour top, there is almost no chance of any staining. You should not put pans straight from the hob or oven onto quartz work surfaces as they could melt or disturb the resin. Like a chocolate bar left in direct sunlight, it becomes soft and pliable. Quartz can be repaired by mixing the resins with a hardener and then polishing it when it is fully cured.

Synthetic worktops. Manufacturers of synthetic worktops include Corian, Hi-Macs, Samsung, Minerelle and Earthstone, to name a few. Synthetic worktops are all similar, but they vary in their make-up. The chemical construction varies slightly between brands, but it doesn't make much difference to you, the customer. As a fabricator, you would notice differences in how easy it is to work with the material to get results. One of the things I love most about synthetic fabrics is that if you can imagine it, you can build and reproduce it.

My first ever design was a reception desk. I made it as a gift for a friend. I got the idea from CD cases. When you stack them staggered, the overhang looks as if it has been suspended. I wanted a worktop to look cantilevered off these staggered boxes. I had no idea how I was going to produce this worktop, but I enjoy problem-solving. Taking a pencil to paper, I broke the design down into the individual parts and then worked out what I would need to do to put these pieces together. As far as I am aware, that reception desk still stands proud in my friend's offices.

Invisible joints. Synthetics are admired because they can be made to look seamless. This makes them popular in hospitals and clinical facilities because they are hygienic and don't harbour germs and bacteria. It is used for cladding buildings because of how it can be shaped and formed, and it's really popular in offices and nightclubs because of the spectacular detailing you can achieve when it is back-lit.

Technically we are not allowed to say 'invisible joints' – we are encouraged to say 'inconspicuous joints'. The reason is that the resins we use to join the worktops will cover a few sheet colours – in other words, there is not an individual colour glue for each top. If you really look for them, you can see the joints. The trick when jointing these worktops is cleanliness: my mantra is clean, clean and clean again before any jointing takes place. You can end up with a black line on a white worktop from something as simple as a bleed from a pencil mark or the printed codes on the back of the sheet.

Synthetic worktops can be repaired easily. Blemishes or cracks can be cut out and then replaced using exactly the same method as jointing the worktops. Always ask to keep any offcuts, especially the ones for the sink and hob cut-outs. Just ask the installer to leave them under your units before they put the plinths on. These sheets are made in batches, so you don't want to be in the situation where you need some repair work done but your batch of worktop is no longer available. Keep the offcuts in a cool dry place and lay them flat to stop them warping.

Appliances

The technology around us is phenomenal. Fridges are becoming intuitive to how we cook, so when you finish an item of food you can scan the bar code and it adds it to a shopping list. You can upload that shopping list to your preferred supermarket and have the shopping delivered to your door. There are fridges with built-in touch screens and speakers so you can stay up-to-date with social media and listen to your favourite play list while you're cooking.

I predict that our cupboards will eventually have scanners. That would mean you could type into your phone, 'What can I make for dinner tonight?', and the cupboard and the fridge could talk to a central database and choose some recipes that you have the ingredients for. This may sound wacky to you or you may be excited by the possibilities.

Appliances are so personal. I have a preferred manufacture that I like to work with but I am always trying to keep pace with the changes in the market. What I have at home is different to what I now have in my showroom.

A few things to consider when picking out your appliances:

- Try before you buy – I like to run demonstration evenings. They are fun and give you first-hand experience of what they can do. I like to find out what sort of recipes my customers like to cook and find appliances that will best suit them.

- Lifestyle – health is becoming more important in our decision making. Steamers are a fantastic addition to complement ovens as they help keep the valuable nutrients in food that get lost when boiling. But they are not just for vegetables. You can do risottos, soups, chicken, fish, and chocolate pudding recipes. Even blanch kale for your morning breakfast smoothies.

- Symmetry – how your appliances look in the design. Consider how you cook now and what would make life easier in your new kitchen. Do you need a single or double oven? Would two single ovens be more beneficial than the conventional double oven which is really an oven and a half? If you are having a steamer, microwave oven or coffee machine which is 450mm in height, are you going to balance it with a 150mm warming drawer so that when placed next to a 600mm high single oven the design looks cohesive?

- Ice cool – Fridges can be a contentious area, especially when family members want different styles. Do you want them to be in-built? Or are you after a large free standing American fridge freezer. American fridges will govern your overall kitchen design as they can only be placed in certain areas in the kitchen. Do you require an ice dispenser? That will certainly sway your decision to go with the American fridge style. Do you require a sub fridge to keep every day essentials while food is stored in a larger fridge?

Water heaters and instant boiling water taps: When the instant boiling water tap was first introduced, it was a Marmite product – you either loved it or hated it. Why do I need to be able to make a cup of tea instantaneously? You might be thinking, 'Oh, Robert, do you know how many kettles I can buy for the price of that instant boiling water tap?' You could buy ten kettles. I know!

Think about it like this. If you buy one cup of coffee a day at a coffee shop, over a year you'll spend more than you would for the instant boiling water tap. But the principle is the same, if you like a hot drink on the way to work. Of course, you can get up a little earlier and make yourself a hot drink to take in a thermos. But if you prefer to rock up to the station, grab one on the go and throw it away when you're done, you're paying for the convenience. You want it when you want it, and not a moment later.

I appreciate that £600 to £700 is a lot to pay for instant boiling water, but it comes back to convenience. If you want to cook some ravioli before you fly out the door to Pilates, do you want to wait for the kettle to boil or did you want that boiling water five minutes ago? Why do more and more offices now install instant boiling water taps at the tea points? Because it stops employees wasting any more time than they need to when they make a cuppa. Whether you're an employer or an employee, all the money in the bank can't buy back time.

Are instant boiling water taps safe for children? In the UK, we would not be able to bring a product to market if it were dangerous. Most of the taps, especially the brand leaders, have built-in safety systems to prevent scalding. For example, you might have to hold a button in or pump the handle twice before turning the tap on. You'll need to get your tap serviced, but you don't drive your car for three years without changing the filter or the oil. If you want your tap to work like it did on day one, stay on top of this. The installer or kitchen supplier can set up a service agreement.

Do you need a water softener? If you live in a soft-water area, oh what a luxury it must be to feel you are bathing in silky flows of H_2O. Unfortunately, I live in a hard-water area and limescale collects around the sinks and bathrooms. What causes hard water and limescale? Metal ions like calcium and magnesium can cause limescale to form. Limescale can foul up the plumbing and cause corrosion, as well as leaving the tell-tale white marks on everything.

If you have hard water, I suggest you avoid black or dark colours for your worktops. Greys are a little more forgiving. It breaks my heart when a client insists on having black in a hard-water area. I love a honed or flamed finish on granite – it looks and feels spectacular. But in a hard-water area it looks great on the day of installation and then limescale gets in the way. You need dedication to stay on top of it.

Equipment – Task

Before deciding on the equipment that you want, answer the following questions:

- Do you live in a hard-water or soft-water area?

- Where are your hob and oven placed? Are they on an outside wall? Can you easily vent the air? Do you need to consider the cost and hassle of ducting?

- How will you heat the room? Underfloor heating or radiators?

- Do you know what appliances you use most and which new ones will assist you better in your new kitchen?

Next steps

DIY – Do it with you, do it for you

When I passed my motorbike test, I knew exactly where my first journey was going to be. My grandma lives on the Dorset coast and I had the route all mapped out. I had written the directions in large font on the computer so I could stick them to the tank and read them on the way down. I got there without a hitch. With a beaming smile and open arms, my grandma greeted me at the door with welcoming arms. The journey was successful because of the clarity I had. I knew exactly where I wanted to be heading, I followed the instructions and executed them to the letter.

Your new dream kitchen will be no different, and this book is your map to your perfect kitchen. Your first question is: where do you want to be with your space?

The redesign

For the least amount of disruption, use the space you have and redesign that area. You know what you have, you can visualise it and you are comfortable with this. You know where the sockets and water services are, and what you would need to do to move them or add new ones. The windows are already in place, so you can tick those off your list. What you might struggle with is finding a fresh approach. If I gave you one of those colouring books for adults, the colours would be completely your choice – you could colour a tree with fresh green leaves for spring or orange and brown for autumn, but there's no getting away from the fact that it's a tree. If I gave you a blank piece of paper you could sketch a sun-kissed beach. The picture is your choice, not someone else's.

When redesigning an existing space, you might fall into the trap of just doing the same thing. If you're going to do that, you might as well keep the units and change the door fronts and worktops.

When Eddie and Sharon approached me they had a good sized space, already open plan, but its original design was a galley-style layout with two parallel runs of kitchen units. Three other designers had created designs for the space based on the same layout. All because of a window that sat below the line of the units. 'Change the window,' I hear you cry, 'it's obvious!' Well, that was my first thought too! This wasn't possible because of a covenant that stated that they couldn't change the external appearance of the house. To solve the problem, I suggested putting the units across the window and getting some graphics that they could stick to the internal glass. They chose an image of a flower box.

Of course, keeping your existing space is perfectly fine, but stay open-minded about design and push the boundaries of what is possible.

The knock-through

The most common way to create an open-plan kitchen is to knock through an adjoining wall to another room to add to the size of the existing kitchen. Nine times out of ten, that room is the dining room or living room. This is the fun bit when we get to pretend we are builders and do the knock. You know the one, when you tap on the wall with your knuckles to see if it's a supporting wall. If it sounds hollow it must be a stud wall and if it doesn't sound hollow it must be a supporting wall, right? If this was an interactive book, here's where you'd see a big fat X light accompanied by the incorrect buzzer noise from a TV game show.

Do not under any circumstances try to be a builder, an architect or a structural engineer. These professionals know their stuff. Plaster that has come away from the wall can make the wall sound hollow. So put your sledgehammer away and get a second – and maybe even a third – opinion. You never know what you are going to find until a more detailed inspection has been carried out.

In any case, the adjoining wall is a small consideration compared with thinking about what you can do with the space. This is closer to the blank piece of paper I mentioned earlier, as you can think of the space you will create as an entirely new area. Where you want to be is the driving force for how we get there.

The extension

The third option, which is becoming ever popular, is to add an extension to your home instead of moving to a larger one. I love to see people investing in their homes to give themselves the lifestyle they want and deserve. You have the house in the area you want, the children are in the school you want, and the local amenities are where you need them. Whatever your reason for staying put and creating that open-plan kitchen and living space, an extension is a great way to do that.

You may be wondering if you will get a return on your investment. I am no estate agent and I can't advise you on the commercial rewards. I've always answered this question as honestly as I dare. I say yes, in the long term you will eventually get a return on the investment of adding an extension to your home. The expression that sits most comfortably with me is to be *impatiently patient*. If you could do something now to improve your situation tommorrow, would you? The rewards will come eventually. Adding a few metres to the back or side of the house can create a fantastic and desirable space, your ultimate blank canvas. If you have accepted that there's going to be some disruption in your home (for example, moving plumbing and electrical services), it will be worth getting the space exactly how you want it.

What about planning permission?

Don't do something without getting permission and then ask for forgiveness. I think at one stage or another, we've all been guilty of this. You thought it would be OK to do something and then it turned out it wasn't. You grovel a little, time passes and you think all is forgiven and forgotten. Sadly, this is not the case. Getting permission for building work is paramount to a successful, stress-free project. Please don't think that if you've spent a whopping amount of money on your project, they'll ruffle your hair and tell you to 'be on your way, you little scamp'. They can tell you to bring the whole thing crashing to the ground. I hate hearing stories like this – please don't let yours be one of them.

The redesign

You shouldn't need any planning permission for this type of work. But if you are planning work in a listed or historic building, you may want to seek some professional advice. Getting these sorts of permissions will add time to your project. A good guideline to follow is to make the changes reversible. That means it is possible to revert to the original fabric, construction and look of the building. This type of work will reduce the disruption to any historic, protected materials.

The knock-through

There are two types of knock-throughs. One is taking down a stud wall that has no load-bearing capacity – that is, removing it does not affect the structure of the building. The other is taking down a load-bearing wall. This could be part of the spine of the building that keeps your home standing up. You might not need planning permission, but you will need to involve building control. Building control is the governing body that ensures that the work has been carried out in line with building regulations and that it meets the minimum standards. Please check with your lead builder to make sure you or they get your project signed off at the relevant stages. Ultimately, if you are the owner and the work doesn't follow the regulations, you could be served with an enforcement notice and asked to re-do the work.

The extension

You might not always need planning permission when building an extension. Your building work might fall within what are called permitted development rights, which does not require planning permission. To add to the confusion, your home may be in what's known as a designated area, which could be a conservation area or a world heritage site. These cover whole areas of Britain, like the Norfolk and Suffolk broads. If your home is in a designated area, you do need planning permission. For the sake of a ten-minute phone call, speak to the planning office and ask for some advice and help. They are not there to trip you up. They want help you as much as they can.

Planning permission will push back your start date by between ten and twelve weeks. This doesn't include the time your architect will need to draw up any plans that the planning office needs to see.

My tips on planning permission:

- **Be a good neighbour.** If you're thinking about building an extension, go and speak to your neighbours. Let them air any concerns they may have. Tell them when you are hoping to start your project. Be aware that if they have young children or they are a little more advanced in life, they may be at home while some of the noisy work is happening. Knowing when the work is happening might help them plan holidays so they can avoid the inconvenience.

- **Speak to the guys at the planning department.** They are lovely people. It takes no time at all to start to build a relationship and tap into their wealth of knowledge.

- **It always takes longer than you expect.** Manage your expectations. I will hold my hand up and acknowledge that I want things to happen straight away, but embrace the wait. Use the extra time to make educated and well-informed decisions. You will want to enjoy the work for many years to come, so you don't want to make rushed choices.

How much are the building costs?

Although I would love to give you a definite answer, this is impossible because everyone's project is different. The only tip I can give you without meeting you and knowing more about your building project is that it will cost more than you think. Whatever number you have in your head, add 20%. Then, any saving you make will bring a smile to your face.

We all love to feel that we are getting good value for money, but in the renovation game you never know what you are going to find, uncover or inherit. The good news is that there's always a solution to every problem you come across. Granted, some inconveniences may require some extra funds, but be optimistic. See inconveniences for what they are – just little speed bumps to get over. With the right team around you, everything is do-able.

The redesign

This can be cost-effective in terms of building work. If you're upgrading your appliances, though, you may want to consult an electrician about getting new electrical supplies from the fuse board. For example, if you're changing from a gas hob to an induction hob, your new hob will need more than a 13-amp supply.

The knock-through

As mentioned in the planning section, there are two types of knock-through and this is reflected in the cost. If you have a load-bearing or structural wall, professional services will need to help remove it. These will include a structural engineer. You can expect to pay between £300 and £600 for this work. Depending on how much you think you are going to remodel this area of your home, you might want to consider using an architect as well.

The extension

You might expect an extension to be the most expensive option. While I agree with you I would also ask, expensive compared with what?

I had a friend drop by the office the other day for a coffee. As we chatted, the conversation turned to where I saw the business in five years. I said I wanted to build a business that could help families all over the country to create lifestyle kitchens. He is a cautious person and asked me how I was going to do that while I was still trying to grow and expand locally. I agreed that my business was still in its infancy. But it takes the same amount of effort to think small as it does to think big. My 'why' will help me drive my ambition to help as many families as I can.

If you chose an extension over a knock-through, would that give you the space you need and create a family dynamic you never had before? Would it help create the lifestyle kitchen you want? Yes, the extension costs are going to be more, but will it give you better results? What value do you put on the benefits you'll get from your investment?

The professional services you'll need will include an architect and a structural engineer. You'll need to consider the cost of applying for and getting planning permission and paying the fee for a building inspector. Some companies offer to bundle these together and co-ordinate the service by making calls and sending emails on your behalf.

A quick way to estimate your budget is to work out how many square metres your extension will be, allowing between £1,600 and £1,900 per square metre. This will not include the cost of the kitchen units, worktops or appliances, but it will give you a good-quality finish throughout. When it comes to financing, personal loans are capped at £25,000. If you need to borrow more than £25,000, you could speak to a mortgage adviser about borrowing money against your home. You can also speak to building societies about a home-improvement loan, which could be up to £200,000.

Who can help design my new space?

When it comes to open-plan kitchens, there are many people available to help you. My clients have found it helpful to bring me in when they first commit to the idea of taking on the project.

Jane and Paul had a builder who recommended my company. They had already had the architectural drawings approved by the planning department. The builder had started the ground works and the first phase of the build, including the drainage. As soon as Paul and Jane had brought us up to speed on their brief and shown us the architect's plans, alarm bells were ringing. The brief was to have a kitchen with a walk-in pantry that backed onto a utility room. The width of the room and the space available to walk through to the pantry was the biggest issue.

The couple had decided on pocket doors (which slide into the partition wall when they are open), which made perfect sense. An open door would have reduced the space even further and with a pantry you want as much vertical storage and as many shelves as possible. As the room wasn't wide enough for any central storage or a butcher's block, all the units had to be positioned along the walls. The pantry was smaller than the utility room. The sink and prep tables in the utility had already been laid out in line with the architect's plans and the plumbing and drainage had been installed. But by moving the sink and prep tables in the utility room, we could increase the space in the pantry.

The knock-on effect to Jane and Paul was that the drainage needed to be moved to suit their preferred layout.

Jane and Paul's architect hadn't made a mistake, but my knowledge of space management and products gave us more opportunities to make the most of the space available. I would liken this to comparing a vet and a doctor. Both are in the business of sustaining life. They keep humans and animals alive to the best of their ability. The similarities are many – hearts, respiratory systems and brain functions. But there are differences in how they must be cared for and worked with.

A kitchen designer and a kitchen planner

The common misunderstanding is that these two types of people are one and the same, like an eggplant and an aubergine. The truth is that they are like chalk and cheese. High-street stores have created expectations that kitchen design should not be paid for. This makes the overall service more appealing to more people, but we both know that the design cost is factored into the kitchen some way or another. One company I know of send out their managers to scour the supermarkets and large goods stores for young adults who they can poach, put on a short training course and call them a designer. They are not designers – at best, they are planners.

Planners understand the software and they know how to produce the images that lead customers to believe that what they have produced looks like a kitchen. But this doesn't translate well in the execution. The fitters will curse the plans because the planners have no concept of the practicalities.

You can make anything look perfect on a computer screen, because on the screen everything works to millimetre precision. If the room is three metres long, logic and the software suggest that you can have five 600mm base units. But no house is perfectly square. In a three-metre alcove, the walls may run outwards, run inwards, or – my favourite – are a trapezium. They might give you the illusion that your kitchen is square, when in fact it could not be further from the truth. That's why at least one of those units should be downsized to allow for equal fillers or infill décor panels. A good rule of thumb is to change a 600mm unit to a 500mm one with two 50mm infill panels.

You may be lucky and get a more worldly planner who has made this mistake and learned from it, but these companies have such a high turnover of staff that you might be working with a new planner. A designer has a much more in-depth understanding of not only the software but also the products and the limitations of the site.

I am lucky to have experience in all the areas of the design journey, from understanding how a chef would want their space, to designing it and installing. Some of the best designers have on-site experience. It is not uncommon to pay a designer for their plans; in fact, I think there is merit in doing that. When we pay for something it sets a clear understanding of expectation. Have you ever bought something online and found that it doesn't arrive on the day you were told? You quite rightly have grounds for compensation, as the company you ordered from have not fulfilled their end of the agreement. Paying a designer will hold them accountable for what they produce.

While design is about interpretation, I also believe it goes hand in hand with a desire to please, thrill and inspire. Your designer should want to give their best because they are being valued for their insights and knowledge. The strength of independent designers is their desire to go over and above for consumers and give them the best customer journey. Independent designers are now becoming an increasingly popular choice.

Fitting and installation tips

Some people think a good fitter can make a bad kitchen look good, and a bad fitter can make a good kitchen look bad. I think there are only two types of fitter – a passionate fitter and a lazy fitter.

When I was employed at my first kitchen company I had no formal training. I was not at college – in fact, I was too old to go, and to send me to college would have cost a small fortune. So what did my employer see in me that told him I was the right guy for him and his company? I had belief and passion. After a month of working for that kitchen company I understood the hierarchy and had got my head around a few of the processes. I wrote my employer an email with my five-year plan for how I was going to become the best at what I did and how I would go about doing it. I had the best completion rate and my ratio for call backs was the smallest in the company. I put my success down to one thing – I asked myself: if I could do it better, would I? That's the difference between the cream of the fitters and the watered-down milk.

Now, anyone can criticise or 'snag' someone's work, there's no way around that. It's no different to a plate of food leaving the kitchen and the diner adding some salt or pepper to his or her meal. While the chef believed it to be perfect, the diner's taste is different. I'm not making excuses – people's tolerances vary. Consistency is what's important. If a fitter is going to do it one way, they should it that way throughout the whole kitchen.

If you have an end panel or décor panel, nine times out of ten the fitter will cut it so it finishes flush with the door. And rightly so. It looks great and it's a lovely simple detail. On the other hand, they might do an infill to the wall as the carcass line, which is set back from door. This, doesn't look very good. Commonly a lazy fitter will not want to have to spend time cutting more material so that the infill can be placed forward, to the door line. Some high-street kitchen shops sell replacement panels. These are not end panels but they provide the same benefits – the plinth has a finished end to stop at and it doesn't have to be mitred and returned the wall. It would always be my choice to use an end panel and align it flush with the door rather than have a replacement end and leave the kitchen looking unfished.

Another classy and subtle finishing touch is to cut a hole in a unit so you can get to a plug for an appliance. For example, you could have one in the cupboard under the sink for a plug from the washing machine or dishwasher. The hole is finished with a plastic cap, known as a cable tidy. You would expect to find these in desks for phone and monitor cables.

Why does this matter? The most important thing is how your kitchen looks and performs, but if a fitter is taking this much care with the bits that you don't see, you know they'll take the utmost care with the bits you do see.

DIY

I don't recommend that you fit your own kitchen, but if you really want to do it I will offer a few suggestions to make your life easier. To be clear, you shouldn't do this type of work if you don't have the skills you need, and you must take the proper precautions and use all, the eye, breathing, ear and hand protection available to you. That said, we can now go ahead.

Fillers and end panels are important, so here are three tips for cutting them neatly.

1. It doesn't matter what jigsaw you have, whether it's from a supermarket or whether it's top of the range from a tool shop. Turn the speed right down. Less is always more. Most jigsaws have speed settings from 1 to 6, with 6 being the fastest. Setting your saw at a speed of 3.5 to 4 is perfect. The problem with turning the speed up is that it makes you want to go faster. If you turn the speed down, you'll focus on the cut, not how quickly you're cutting.

2. Let the blade do the work. I prefer to cut downwards, so that gravity does its thing and you have no need to push. You just need to watch where you are going.

3. Cut from the back, not the front of the panel. Make sure you can see the blade, not the main body of the jigsaw. Depending on the quality of the jigsaw, the sharpness of the blade and even the thickness of the material you are cutting through will affect the line you take. Jigsaw blades tend to wander. Think of it like cutting along a line with a pair of scissors – you cut what you see and make the adjustments as and when you need to. Cutting like this works just as well with a jigsaw. If you are unsure, there are some more tips on my website.

4. When measuring to cut the panels, measure and cut the height first and then measure and cut the width or depth. If you do it in reverse, you are likely to come unstuck. If you cut it to the right depth first, and the floor runs out (that is, it's higher or lower from front to back) you have no scope to make the corrections needed. The beautiful cut you've made around the skirting will be in the wrong place when you lower the height of the panel to make it touch the floor. If you have shaped skirting then all your indents and knobbles will be in the wrong places. Avoid the temptation – cut the bottom first and then scribe the

panel back to the wall. For more details on how to do this, visit my website.

Do you need a project manager?

The simplest way to decide whether you should run your own project or have a project manager is ask this question: How much do you value your time? That was meant to sound as bullish as you read it. If you're the type of person who gets the car washed at a garage, has groceries delivered or has a gardener, I would suggest that you get a project manager. Because you value your time.

Time is finite. With all the money in the world you cannot buy it back, but you can pay for it in advance. A project manager is there to take the stress and strain, co-ordinate the work and solve problems as they happen. All of my projects are about making the customer journey smoother and the experience easier. A project manager is about having one number to call, at any time, on any day of the year. If I have a customer who has a burning question at 11pm on a Sunday, they don't have to wait until 9am on Monday to ask. They can do it then and there. Any renovation project is a big deal, and why shouldn't you be able to get hold of your project manager whenever you need them? If I'm needed for a five-minute phone call when my client's on the other side of the world in a different time zone, I'm going to be there.

If you love a challenge and you have the temperament to handle each problem that comes up, I salute your courage. Here are a few tips and tricks to help you stay on top of the situation.

- **Build rapport.** Every tradesperson or sub-contractor loves to be appreciated. Who doesn't? At the very least, offer them a cup of tea or coffee. If you want real leverage, leave a packet of biscuits. It's obvious, but it will help you build a better rapport with your contractors. Then, when you need the electrician to look at the dodgy light switch in the loft, they'll be more willing to want to help you in return.

- **The price is the price.** Always agree all the costs up front. Cover yourself and get a detailed quote from the sub-contractors. This should set out what it includes and what it doesn't – don't have any grey areas. If you do, they'll sit there waiting to pounce and put a spanner in the works. It's in everyone's interest to agree a price. Allow the contractor to put their price to you and respect their professional opinion.

- **Avoid paying a day rate.** Day work can encourage rogues to drag out the job for longer than needed. If the contractor says it's £400 for two days, don't ask for money back if they finish at one o'clock on the second day. The price is set and they have carried out the work. It's the same the other way around – if the sub-contractor comes back to you at the end of the second day to say they're going to need a third day, you won't want to pay any more. Basing the cost of the work on price rather than days avoids this. You accept the contractor's evaluation of the work needed, and they have to swallow the cost of anything they did not allow for in the written quote.

- **Use a professional.** I have a saying, 'everyone's a kitchen fitter'. I've often been told, 'Oh, my dad fitted mine,' or 'My friend did mine'. That's great, and I'm not against anyone that wants to have a go. If you have the confidence, then why not? But anyone can get themselves in over their head; a true trade professional knows how to get themselves out.

- **Watch out for rogue traders.** Rogue traders cut corners because they don't know how to do the job or they want to save time or money. A professional can make quick, educated, decisions to get the job done correctly and safely to a high standard.

- **Use a specialist, not a generalist.** Using a specialist is a better use of resources. You wouldn't get a butcher to bake you a cake. Their sausage rolls may be renowned throughout the village, but they're not branching out to sell you triple chocolate fudge gateaux. There are some great carpenters about, but kitchen fitters are specialists. I have no formal training as a carpenter; I don't hide it and have no shame announcing it. I can't cut a roof in, and I've never tried. I can fit an internal door but I couldn't do it as quickly as a carpenter. I don't need to – that's what they do.

- **Don't ask the builder to fit your kitchen.** I would guess that almost every builder who fits a kitchen gets a specialist fitter to come and do the worktop joints. A close friend of mine is a builder, and we have a rule – I won't tell him how to build a brick wall and he won't tell me how to fit a kitchen. We stick to our own skills, and it works perfectly. We each know how the other works and we end up complementing each other's work.

Conclusions

You've taken a look at the seven mistakes that plague most kitchen designs and the seven solutions so you won't fall into the traps. We've gone into detail with my **HOME** system, taking into consideration **H**armony, **O**rganisation, **M**ood and **E**quipment. Finally, we looked at your next steps. Now you are ready to start making decisions.

A home is where we make our memories. Make your house into a home with a lifestyle kitchen. I'd love to help you, but I don't have the time to help everyone. That's why I put so much information into this book.

Whether you decide to go it alone or call me for advice, remember that when you know your 'why', anything is possible. You're only a phone call away from your dream kitchen and a happy, harmonious home.

Acknowledgements

I wanted to thank my wife Catherine first and foremost. Without your support I could have never followed my passion and chased my dream. We have shared ups and downs and you have never stopped encouraging me. Thank you for giving me two beautiful daughters in Francesca and Rhiannon. You three are my Why. Why it's important to be the best version of myself.

Thank you to my family and friends who have paid constant attention to my career and have been willing me to succeed.

Thank you to Helen, Alex and Flo, to whom I entrusted with the beta versions of the book.

To all my mentors: TT, Grant, Tony, Daniel, Robert, Arnold,

Keith and Eric, who have shared their wisdom with me and inspired my journey.

To Lucy, Joe and Debs, who helped me turn my book into a reality. You three helped me put my voice into print. You guys knew how hard writing was for me and didn't stop encouraging me until the end.

To all my amazing customers that entrusted me to shape their home and give them their lifestyle kitchen.

The Author

Robert's passion for kitchens began when he left school at age 16 and trained to be a chef. He worked at the prestigious Hertfordshire country club, Brockett Hall, across three kitchens, and learned from some wonderfully talented head chefs. He not only learned to cook but also  learned some valuable lessons about creativity, presentation and quality. In his next job, Robert began working with a kitchen-fitting company, where he discovered a natural flair for carpentry and took great pride in the quality of finish for every job he worked on.

At the age of 28, Robert decided the time was right to set up his own kitchen business. He knew his experience of working in a kitchen and fitting kitchens gave him a unique perspective on the best design, layout and features that would make his kitchen designs truly great.

On 22 February 2014, Catherine, Robert's wife, gave birth to Jacob. He was still-born with a fatal anomaly called lethal skeletal dysplasia. This untreatable condition results in babies being born prematurely or still-born, or dying from respiratory failure shortly after birth. Catherine and Robert spent the night with Jacob before making the decision to donate his body to medical research, as they wanted some good to come from their heartbreaking situation.

Through their own loss the couple re-evaluated their lives, and were determined to honour Jacob's memory. Surrounded by their family, who offered support at that difficult time, it became clear to them that they could help to bring other families together by focusing on open-plan living spaces. They felt that re-branding the kitchen business, with Jacob's name at the helm, was a great way to achieve this. In the years since 2014, the couple have gone on to have a beautiful healthy baby girl, Francesca, and are expecting another baby this September.

The business was re-branded as Jacob Roberts Interiors, with the vision to offer kitchens with family-inspired living at the heart of every design. It is this vision and the importance of family that drive Robert's stunning designs. He specialises in open-plan living and, along with his trusted trade partners, he is able to offer design, fitting and full project-management services, tailored to his customers' needs.

To find out more about Robert's work, and to get in touch, go to:

www.jacob-roberts.co.uk
www.robertjguinan.com
Instagram. Robertjguinan
Twitter @robertjguinan
Facebook. robertjguinan

Lightning Source UK Ltd.
Milton Keynes UK
UKHW02f1204120118
316013UK00001B/2/P